Scepticism and the
Possibility of Knowledge

Scepticism and the Possibility of Knowledge

A. C. GRAYLING

continuum

Continuum UK
The Tower Building, 11 York Road, London SE1 7NX

Continuum US
80 Maiden Lane, Suite 704, New York, NY 10038

www.continuumbooks.com

First published 2008

British Library Cataloguing-in-Publication Data
A catalogue record for this book is available from the British Library.

ISBN 9-781-8470-6173-7

Typeset by Kenneth Burnley, Wirral, Cheshire
Printed and bound by The Cromwell Press, Wiltshire

Contents

Introduction

My aim in the following pages is to show how a correct anatomization of scepticism about the possibility of knowledge suggests appropriate responses to it. I do this by considering two sets of arguments from two major anti-sceptical orientations – Berkeley and Russell in the Cartesian tradition, Quine and Wittgenstein in different versions of a naturalistic tradition – to see why the strategy I suggest has merits. In their different ways the two kinds of anti-sceptical strategy I examine are not so much incorrect as incomplete, and as such can be seen as constituting aspects of a strategy which I suggest is the right overall one, prompting one to think that what we have in this debate, thus viewed, is similar to the case of the blind men patting an elephant – one the trunk, another a leg, the third an ear or a flank, each describing one particular bit and not realizing that the bits connect.

I came to think that the bits connect in the way I suggest rather early in what has been a long-standing interest in scepticism and cognitive foundations in epistemology. It began when discussing Kant with P. F. Strawson, and with

A. J. Ayer the concept of an analytical reconstruction of the basis of empirical knowledge, while I was a student and then a young teacher at Oxford. The ideas thus prompted resulted first in my doctoral work at Oxford and in my early book *The Refutation of Scepticism* (Duckworth, 1985). Originating versions of the components of this present book first appeared as papers written at various times and published in various places in the years between then and now. They arose out of the endeavour to develop and apply the transcendentalist view argued for in that early book, whose strategy and conclusions I stand by. In bringing together this work now I do so in full consciousness of the continuing recent debate about epistemological scepticism – my own work has appeared in collections of papers bodying forth some of these developments – which I do not directly address here because the task in hand is expressly one of looking at ways certain key approaches in the tradition inform the line of thought I have been working out, and which stands at a sharp angle to some of what has been more recently argued.

This last is not a merely rhetorical remark. The influential lines of debate about scepticism and the possibility of knowledge forged in recent years by Michael Williams (notably) and other contributors including Quassim Cassam, offer very interesting and importantly different perspectives from the one offered here.[1] Williams' diagnosis of the sources of scep-

---

1   See Michael Williams, *Unnatural Doubts: Epistemological Realism and the Basis of Scepticism*, Princeton University Press,

ticism – that it is an artefact of 'epistemological realism' having it that knowledge consists in the achievement of the right kind of objective epistemic relations – suggests to him a contextualist alternative that carries the marks of Rorty's influence. Cassam argues against the idea that the conditions of knowledge body forth structural features of human cognitive capacities. Both these views, and the movements in epistemology they represent, differ in both premises and ambition from what I argue below. Hence, rather than add to my studies of representative types of Cartesian and naturalistic epistemologies by including examinations of these ideas, I leave the matter to direct comparison of strategy. If what follows issues in a perspective of merit, that will itself constitute both a contribution to the current debate and an answer to the alternative proposals made in it.

There are fashions in philosophy, in the sense that a given topic or area of debate consumes interest and discussion for a while, before the spotlight of attention moves on to another area. Theory of knowledge occupied, or at least shared, centre-stage for a long time in technical philosophy, from the seventeenth century to the mid-twentieth century,

---

1996; Quassim Cassam, *The Possibilty of Knowledge*, Oxford University Press, 2007. Cassam's paper 'Can Transcendental Epistemology Be Naturalised?' (*Philosophy* 78 [2003], pp. 181–203) pushes directly counter to the direction of argument in my discussion here, especially in Part III.

before being supplanted by philosophy of language, then philosophy of mind, and the subsequent merging of the two. My own first impulses to philosophy were epistemological. In the tradition of Descartes and Russell, and indeed prompted by examining their views, I was driven to explore the nature of knowledge and its limits, and to see what can be known with certainty, and what relation such foundations, if any, bear to the edifice both of quotidian knowledge and of the more consciously organized bodies of theory constitutive of the natural and social sciences. The first task – descrying the structure of quotidian knowledge – not only retains a vital intrinsic interest, but is arguably central to understanding other sets of relations between thought and experience and the domains over which they range (for focal cases: the spatio–temporal domain, the domain of abstract objects, and the fictional domain). To get clear about the one that has traditionally occupied the centre of attention – the domain of spatio–temporal particulars and events involving them (or which constitute them: but this metaphysical aspect is not addressed here) – has been a primary focus on the technical side of my interest. This has involved thinking about what the sceptical challenge in theory of knowledge requires of us in response, and how that response integrates with intuitions about the other sets of relations between thought and experience and their targets – such as referring to things, theorizing about them, making assertions about them, thinking of them, perceiving them, representing them to oneself: all overlapping and interconnected relations between (for want of a quicker phrase, *pace* the reservations of Rorty and others who repudiate the idea of *relations* in the case altogether) mind and world or worlds.

It is not possible to give an adequate account of any of these relations without having views in philosophical logic, specifically about meaning and reference, assertion, truth and the question of realism. I address some aspects of these, in ways that directly relate to the concerns here, in a companion volume *Truth, Meaning and Realism* (Continuum, 2007).

The study of scepticism might be said to define epistemology. As the enquiry into the nature and sources of knowledge, epistemology's twofold concern is to identify and examine the conditions whose satisfaction will amount to knowledge. Familiarly, one of these crucial conditions is justification. The problems facing the justification of knowledge-claims can best and most powerfully be described by framing them as sceptical challenges, meeting which – if possible – will certify that we are at least sometimes entitled to make claims to knowledge.

Given the centrality of the question of justification in epistemology, and given that the work required of justification is defined by sceptical challenges to our claims to know, it is essential to get the nature of scepticism itself right. A primary task in what follows is to describe the anatomy of scepticism correctly, restricting attention for the purposes of this study to what was once standardly called 'our knowledge of the external world'; that is, empirical knowledge (including science). I argue that the anatomization I offer suggests what form a response to scepticism should take. As a necessary adjunct to arguing for such a response in detail, and as preparatory to any project that seeks to do so, I characterize and discuss, as noted, two species each of two genera of responses to scepticism in the epistemological tradition: two rather different 'Cartesian' responses, offered by Berkeley and Russell (Part I), and two rather different 'naturalistic' responses, offered by Wittgenstein and Quine (Part II).

The first two are 'Cartesian' in accepting a premise fundamental to the Cartesian tradition in epistemology; namely, that the proper starting point for enquiry into the basis of our knowledge of the world is the private data of consciousness ('ideas' or 'sense data'), from which the existence and character of outer objects have to be inferred, or which in some way have to provide a basis for or constraint on claims about outer objects (using this expression generically for the targets in the spatio–temporal realm). Berkeley's endeavour is classic in this tradition; Russell discovered the impossibility of the endeavour, as thus austerely construed, in the course of trying to work it out for himself. But he had missed a trick earlier, I argue, in failing to see that there is a different way of providing foundations for empirical knowledge in an account of their necessary cognitive conditions, one that he had himself ventured in discussing the foundations of geometry. This belongs in Part I under the 'Cartesian' label because, although Russell's endeavour here is palpably Kantian, one aspect of the Kantian endeavour itself is, in the meaning of the term here given, 'Cartesian' as requiring the foundations of knowledge to be, in a sense rather like Putnam's, 'in the head'. But a virtue of the Kantian approach is that it is only one aspect of it which is so; for it very naturally, as if via a schematism of its own, relates to the other approach here canvassed, namely, naturalism.

The two examples of naturalism (Part II) are of notably different kinds. Quine's naturalized epistemology starts from acceptance of the deliverances of our best current scientific theories about the world, and premises them in the account we give of how we get both those theories and our general empirical beliefs. At one level he is obviously right: there is a rich account of how we acquire empirical knowledge in the psychology of learning. But the descriptive story is not by itself a justificatory story, given that to think that the former obviates the necessity for the latter is to fail to grasp the significance of the sceptical challenge that gives the justificatory task its point.

Wittgenstein's views in 'On Certainty' turn on the idea of there being beliefs (those expressed by certain of the 'grammatical' or 'hinge' propositions on which the sense of a given stretch of language turns) which are indispensable to thinking or talking in the given way. The unfinished nature of 'On Certainty' does not yield a finished statement of such a view, but it has interesting connections to naturalistic strands in Hume and to some extent Kant, and these are of central relevance here as implied and applied in my own suggestion about the right approach.

Profiting from the lessons learned in these excursions, and leaving them largely to speak for themselves, in the final part (Part III) I turn to the question of describing scepticism correctly and outlining the direction in which an adequate response to it should go. In essentials the argument under this latter head is that our knowledge claims are domiciled in a justificatory inferential structure, in which certain beliefs of relatively greater generality are used as assumptions in establishing certain beliefs of relatively lesser generality; and that the scheme as a whole rests on a specifiable set of beliefs which serve as undischargeable assumptions of greatest generality for it. Sceptical challenge has then to be reformulated as a challenge to show either that the scheme as a whole is the only possible one (perhaps by means of anti-relativistic arguments like Davidson's as expressed in 'On the Very Idea of a Conceptual Scheme') or that even if there were possible alternative schemes, that its employment is inherently or (more weakly) pragmatically justified nevertheless.

Acknowledgements

My thanks are due to the editors of the collections in which these papers first appeared: Steven Luper (ed.), *The Skeptics: Contemporary Essays* (Ashgate: London) 2003; A. Orenstein and P. Kotatko (eds), *Knowledge, Language and Logic: Questions for Quine* (Boston Studies in the Philosophy of Science Vol. 210) (Boston) 1999; Nicholas Griffin (ed.), *The Cambridge Companion to Bertrand Russell* (Cambridge University Press) 2003; K. Winkler, *The Cambridge Companion to Berkeley* (Cambridge University Press); Stephen Hetherington, *Epistemology Futures* (Oxford University Press) 2006.

PART I

CARTESIAN RESPONSES

CHAPTER 1

Berkeley's Argument for Immaterialism

Berkeley's philosophical view is often described as an argument for 'immaterialism', by which is meant a denial of the existence of matter (or more precisely, *material substance*.) But he also, famously, argued in support of three further theses. He argued for idealism, the thesis that mind constitutes the ultimate reality. He argued that the existence of things consists in their being perceived. And he argued that the mind which is the substance of the world is a single infinite mind – in short, God. These are four different theses, but they are intimately connected in Berkeley's presentation of them, the arguments for the first three sharing most of their premises and steps. My chief purpose in what follows is to give an account of these arguments, their interactions, and the assumptions and methods underlying them. Doing so makes their strengths and weaknesses both conspicuous and perspicuous.

Berkeley's philosophical aim in arguing for these theses is to refute two kinds of scepticism. One is epistemological scepticism, which says that we cannot know the true nature of things because (familiarly) certain perceptual relativities and psychological contingencies oblige us to distinguish appearance from reality in such a way that knowledge of the latter is at least problematic and at worst impossible. The other is theological scepticism, which Berkeley calls 'atheism' and which in his view includes not only views that deny the existence of a deity outright, but also Deism, for which the universe subsists without a deity's continual creative activity. In opposing the first scepticism, Berkeley took himself to be defending common sense and eradicating 'causes of error and difficulty in the sciences'. In opposing the second, he took himself to be defending religion.

The attack on theological scepticism is effected on a metaphysical rather than doctrinal level in P and D.[1] Doctrinal questions receive more attention in such later writings as *Alciphron*. But in one important respect Berkeley saw his views as a fundamental contribution to natural theology, in

---

1   I use the following abbreviations: P for *A Treatise Concerning the Principles of Human Knowledge*, D for *Three Dialogues between Hylas and Philonous*, V for *A New Theory of Vision*, VV for *A New Theory of Vision . . . Vindicated*, C for *Philosophical Commentaries*, DeM for *De Motu*, A for *Alciphron* and S for *Siris*. P20 means *Principles* paragraph 20; 3D200 means the third *Dialogue between Hylas and Philonous* p. 200 in the Luce-Jessop edition (whose pagination is recorded in the Michael Ayers *Everyman* edition also).

that he thought they constitute a powerful new proof of the existence of a God.

Berkeley takes the root of scepticism to be the opening of a gap between experience and the world, forced by theories of ideas like Locke's which involve 'supposing a twofold existence of the objects of sense, the one *intelligible*, or in the mind, the other real and without the mind' (P86). Scepticism arises because

> for so long as men thought that *real* things subsisted without the mind, and that their knowledge was only
> so far forth *real* as it was conformable to *real things*, it follows, they could not be certain they had any real knowledge at all. For how can it be known, that the things which are perceived, are conformable to those which are not perceived, or exist without the mind? (P86)

The nub of the problem is that if we are acquainted only with our own perceptions, and never with the things which are supposed to lie beyond them, how can we hope for knowledge of those things, or even be justified in asserting their existence?

Berkeley's predecessors talked of *qualities* inhering in *matter* and causing ideas in us which *represent* or even *resemble* those qualities. *Matter* or *material substance* is a technical concept in metaphysics, denoting a supposed corporeal basis underlying the qualities of things. Berkeley was especially troubled by the un-empiricist character of this view. If we are to be consistent in our empiricist principles, he asked, how can we tolerate the concept of something which by definition is empirically undetectable, lying hidden behind the perceptible qualities of things as their supposed basis or support? If the concept of matter cannot be defended, we must find a different account of experience and knowledge. Berkeley summarizes his diagnosis of the source of scepticism, and signals the positive theory he has in response to it, in a pregnant remark in C: 'the supposition that things are distinct from Ideas takes away all real Truth, & consequently brings in a Universal Scepticism, since all our knowledge is confin'd barely to our own Ideas' (C606).

A point that requires immediate emphasis is that Berkeley's denial of the existence of matter is not a denial of the existence of the external world and the physical objects it contains, such as tables and chairs, mountains and trees. Nor does Berkeley hold that the world exists only because it is thought of by any one or more finite minds. In one sense of the term 'realist', indeed, Berkeley is a realist, in holding that the existence of the physical world is independent of finite minds, individually or collectively. What he argues instead is that its existence is not independent of Mind.

Berkeley's answer to scepticism, therefore, is to deny that there is a gap between experience and the world – in his and Locke's terminology: between ideas and things – by asserting that things *are* ideas. The argument is stated with admirable

6

concision in P1–6, its conclusion being the first sentence of P7: 'From what has been said, it follows, that there is not any other substance than *spirit*, or that which perceives.' All the rest of P, D and parts of his later writings, consist in expansion, clarification and defence of this thesis. The argument is as follows.

Berkeley begins in Lockean fashion by offering an inventory: the 'objects of human knowledge' are 'either ideas actually imprinted on the senses, or such as are perceived by attending to the passions and operations of the mind, or lastly ideas formed by help of memory and imagination, either compounding, dividing, or barely representing those originally perceived in the aforesaid ways'. Ideas of sense – colours, shapes and the rest – are 'observed to accompany each other' in certain ways; 'collections' of them 'come to be marked by one name, and so to be reputed one thing', for example an apple or tree (P1).

Besides these ideas there is 'something which knows or perceives them'; this 'perceiving, active being is what I call *mind, spirit, soul* or *myself*', and it is 'entirely distinct' from the ideas it perceives (P2).

It is, says Berkeley, universally allowed that our thoughts, passions and ideas of imagination do not 'exist without the mind'. But it is 'no less evident that the various sensations or ideas imprinted on the sense, however blended or combined together (that is, whatever objects they compose) cannot exist otherwise than in a mind perceiving them' (P3).

From these claims it follows that the gap between things and ideas vanishes; for if things are collections of qualities, and qualities are sensible ideas, and sensible ideas exist only in mind, then what it is for a thing to exist is for it to be perceived – in Berkeley's phrase: to be is to be perceived: *esse est percipi*.

For what is said of the absolute [i.e. mind-independent] existence of unthinking things [i.e. ideas or collections of ideas] without any relation to their being perceived, that seems perfectly unintelligible. Their *esse* is *percipi*, nor is it possible that they should have any existence, out of the minds or thinking things which perceive them. (P3)

Berkeley knows that this claim is surprising, so he remarks that although people think that sensible objects like mountains and houses have an 'absolute', that is, perception-independent, existence, reflection on the points just made shows that this is a contradiction. 'For what', he asks, 'are the aforementioned objects but the things we perceive by sense, and what do we perceive besides our own ideas or sensations; and is it not plainly repugnant [illogical, contradictory] that any of these or any combination of them should exist unperceived?' (P4).

The source of the belief that things can exist apart from perception of them is the doctrine of 'abstract ideas', which

Berkeley attacks in his Introduction to P. Abstraction consists in separating things which can only be separated in thought but not in reality, for example the colour and the extension of a surface; or which involves noting a feature common to many different things, and attending only to that feature and not its particular instantiations – in this way we arrive at the 'abstract idea' of, say, redness, apart from any particular red object (P Intro. 6–17). Abstraction is a falsifying move; what prompts the 'common opinion' about houses and mountains is that we abstract existence from perception, and so come to believe that things can exist unperceived. But because things are ideas, and because ideas only exist if perceived by minds, the notion of 'absolute existence without the mind' (i.e. without reference to mind) is a contradiction (P5).

So, says Berkeley, to say that things exist is to say that they are perceived, and therefore 'so long as they are not perceived by me, or do not exist in my mind or that of any created spirit, they must either have no existence at all, or else subsist in the mind of some eternal spirit' (P6). And from this the conclusion it follows that 'there is not any other substance than *spirit*, or that which perceives' (P7).

In sum, the argument is this: the things we encounter in episodes of perceptual experience – apples, stones, trees – are collections of 'ideas'. Ideas are the immediate objects of awareness. To exist they must be perceived; they cannot exist 'without the mind'. Therefore mind is the substance of the world.

Berkeley's defence of this argument from P7 onwards reveals the machinery that drives it, consisting of the interplay between three crucial commitments and the application of an analytic method which requires us to recognize three different levels of explanation – whose own interrelations, in turn, are pivotal to his case.[2]

Let us take the question of the three levels first. Berkeley distinguishes between 'strict', 'speculative' or 'philosophical' ways of understanding matters, and ordinary or 'vulgar' ways of doing so. When we 'think with the wise' we find it necessary to give explanations at what I shall label 'level 1' and 'level 3'. When we 'talk with the vulgar' we do so at 'level 2' (see, e.g., P34–40, esp. P37; 45–8, 3D234–5, C274).

Level 1 concerns the *phenomenology* of experience, consisting of the data of sensory awareness in the form of minima of colour, sound and so for the other senses. Level 2 concerns the *phenomena* of experience – the tables, trees and so forth that we see and touch in the normal course of perception. The phenomenological level (call it level 1) is apparent to us only on a 'strict and speculative' examination of experience. Level 2 phenomena are constituted by level 1 data – not reductively, but mediated in a way revealed by a third, meta-

---

2   I deal with the commitments and the three-level analysis in A. C. Grayling, *Berkeley: The Central Arguments*, Duckworth, 1986; see esp. pp. 22–49, but *passim* for their application.

physical level of explanation (level 3), which describes the causal–intentional activity of mind (ultimately: of an infinite mind) in producing the level 1 data and the level 2 world constituted for us by the organization, coherence and character of the level 1 data (P25–9, 51–2, 2D216).

The analysis can be illustrated by Berkeley's account of causality, which is fundamental to his thesis (P25–9, 51–2, 2D216). At level 3 the world is described as consisting of spirits (minds) and their ideas. Spirits are active, ideas inert. What we take at level 2 to be a case of natural causality – the heat of a fire causing water in a kettle to boil – is, strictly, a succession of individual ideas (composed of level 1 data) caused in us by God (level 3) in such a way that the regularity and consistency of their relations establishes in us a custom of thinking in the familiar level 2 way. This application of the distinction of levels provides, moreover, the basis of the proto-Positivistic philosophy of science sketched by Berkeley later in P (P86–117).

It is a common mistake among commentators to describe Berkeley as a phenomenalist. The distinction of levels shows why they are wrong. Briefly, classical phenomenalism is the view that physical objects are ('logical') constructions out of actual and possible sense-data. The modal adjectives in that sentence serve to explain how the desk in my study exists when not currently being perceived, by showing that we take as true a counterfactual conditional stating that the desk could be perceived if any perceiver

were suitably placed. That indeed defines what, on the phenomenalist view, it is for such objects to exist: namely, as at
least enduring possibilities of perception. An essential commitment of phenomenalism, therefore, is that certain counterfactuals are to be taken as barely (that is, non-reductively)
true; which says, in material mode, that the world contains
irreducible possibilia.

Berkeley's view is completely different. The *esse est percipi*
principle requires that a thing must be perceived – actually
perceived – in order to exist. The perceivability of my desk
when it is not currently being perceived (by a finite mind) is
therefore cashed in terms of its actually being perceived (by
an infinite mind). In phenomenalism there are only levels 1
and 2. It is a familiar problem for phenomenalism that level
2 cannot be reduced to level 1 without remainder, and that
therefore level 1 can only be sufficient for level 2 if suitably
supplemented. The supplement is acceptance of the bare
truth of appropriate counterfactuals (and thus an ontology of
possibilia). This exacts a high price for the explanatory shortfall. But for Berkeley there is no such shortfall; his third level
of explanation shows how level 1 constitutes level 2, and
simultaneously gives us a simple account of counterfactuals
by having their truth-conditions fully statable in indicative
terms: 'If I were in my study I would see my desk' is true just
as the case 'My desk is perceived by the infinite mind' is true
(= 'The desk exists'). So on Berkeley's view, possibility is
relative to finite minds only – for the infinite mind whatever

is, is actual. (Whether any of it is also necessary is of course a different and further matter.)[3]

Many of the difficulties standardly alleged in Berkeley's argument vanish when understood in light of the three-level analysis. Illustrations of this occur in due place below.

As noted, three crucial commitments interact with the distinction-of-levels thesis to underwrite Berkeley's argument. They are commitments to empiricism, to the epistemic character of modality, and, as we have already seen, to the vacuity of the notion of abstract ideas. It might be more accurate to describe the two first as commitments and the third as the conclusion of an argument; but because the two first are premises of that argument, and because all three powerfully combine in the process of refuting scepticism and establishing spirit as the only possible substance, it is convenient to take them together.

Berkeley is a rigorous empiricist; we are not entitled to assert, believe or regard as meaningful anything not justified by experience.[4] The constraint is austerely applied: level 2 is exhaustively explained by level 1 under government of the level 3 causal–intentional story (see, e.g., P38). It might

---

3 Grayling, *Berkeley*, pp. 95–117.

4 The nuance to the effect that no belief or concept is contentful unless *either* acquired by *or* applicable to experience describes a form of empiricism that Berkeley would doubtless accept: but this is not his way of putting things.

appear that Berkeley is less rigorous in his empiricism than Hume because he introduces the notion of 'notions'[5] to explain our knowledge of spirit (other minds and God), which seems expressly to involve a non-sensuous epistemic source, and therefore to conflict with his notebook commitment to the strong principle *nihil est in intellectu quod non prius fuit in sensu* (C779). But we should allow Berkeley at least as much latitude as Locke claims in countenancing intellectual sources of experience. In this sense notions are the counterpart of 'ideas' in Berkeley's sense (mental contents) in the experience of encountering minds through a certain class of their effects. Of course, the ideas that constitute the world are the effects of God's causal influence on our sensory modalities, and are therefore encountered as level 2 physical objects in the standard way. But Berkeley argues that from the character of these ideas and their relations we grasp something further: that a particular sort of mind wills them (this is part of his argument for taking it that the world's substance is a deity somewhat of the personal type offered in revealed religion).[6] Parallel reasoning applies to finite spirits. In DeM, Berkeley discusses the kind of experience that has self-awareness as its object; he calls it 'reflexion' (DeM40).

---

5   Named as such only in the second edition of P, but importantly present from the outset: see the first sentence of P1 where 'ideas of reflection' occur second on the list.

6   The argument is deeply flawed: I discuss it at length in Grayling, *Berkeley*, pp. 183–203.

14

But at P27 and elsewhere we learn that we have knowledge of spirit by its effects, and infer therefore that notions too are the objects of awareness: a second-order awareness, so to speak, consisting in grasp of the significance of ideas acquired in the standard sensory way. The signal point is that without experience *as such* we do not come by notions; so Berkeley's empiricism is unequivocal (P22, 1D200).[7]

The second and third commitments – that possibility is an epistemic concept, viz. *conceivability*; and that there are no abstract ideas – arise from the first (P Intro. 9 et. seq., P4, 1D177, 3D194).[8] His chief form of argument is indeed a conceivability argument: we cannot conceive colour apart from extension, ideas apart from mind, existence apart from perception (P4, 7, P Intro. 8, 9). In both cases the dependence on the empirical commitment is direct. Concepts lack content unless they are empirically derived; the thesis is forcefully

---

7   In Grayling, *Berkeley*, p. 28 I had characterized Berkeley as less thorough-going in his empiricism than Hume because of the apparently ambivalent status of notions. This marks a development of view.

8   And see Grayling, *Berkeley*, pp. 28–40. I shall not rehearse the detailed considerations that show Berkeley's epistemic rendering of possibility to be persuasive – it is a commitment shared widely by his contemporaries – but I should mention that 'conceivability' and 'imaginability' are to be sharply distinguished, the former being strictly controlled by empirical constraints on content, the latter consisting in something like the free play of fancy.

stated in V where Berkeley asks whether it is possible for anyone 'to frame in his mind a distinct abstract idea of visible extension or figure exclusive of all colour: and on the other hand, whether he can conceive colour without visible extension?' and replies, 'For my own part, I must confess I am not able to attain so great a nicety of abstraction: in a strict sense, I see nothing but light and colours, with their several shades and variations' (V130). To 'frame in the mind' is to conceive; the 'strict sense' is the level 1 or phenomenological sense; concepts of extension and figure therefore derive their content wholly from their experiential source, namely, visual minima of 'light and colour'.

There is an important point to be noted at this juncture, anticipated in the presentation given above of Berkeley's P1–7 argument. It is that where Berkeley uses his habitual locution 'without the mind' we do better to use 'without reference to mind'. The point of this recommendation is illustrated by what is at stake in contemporary debates about 'realism' and 'anti-realism'. In this connection realism is the claim that the entities in a given domain exist independently of knowledge or experience of them. The anti-realist denies this. One way of sketching why he denies it is offered by the idiom of relations. Thus recast, realism is the view that the relation between thought or experience and their objects is contingent or external, in the sense that description of neither relatum essentially involves reference to the other. On the anti-realist's view, to take the thought–object relation as external is a mistake at least for the direction object-to-thought, because any account of the content of thoughts about things, and in particular the individuation of thoughts about things, essentially involves reference to the things thought about – this is the force of the least that can be said in favour of notions of broad content. So realism appears to offer a peculiarly hybrid relation: external in the direction thought-to-things, internal in the direction things-to-thought. It is a short step for the anti-realist to argue that thought about (perception of, theories of) things is always and inescapably present in, and therefore conditions, any full account of the things thought about; the poorly worded 'Master Argument' in Berkeley, aimed at showing that one cannot conceive of an unconceived thing, is aimed at making just that elementary point (P23, 1D200).[9] The best example of such a view is afforded by the Copenhagen interpretation of quantum theory, in which descriptions of quantum phenomena are taken *essentially* to involve reference to observers and conditions of observation. Such a view does not constitute a claim that the phenomena are caused by observations of them; no more does anti-realism claim this in respect of the subject-matters in which it argues its case, for it is not a metaphysical but an epistemological thesis. This is why anti-realism is not idealism, for idealism is a metaphysical thesis about the constitution of reality

---

9   See Grayling, *Berkeley*, pp. 113–17.

(namely: that reality is mental), not, as anti-realism is, an epistemological thesis about the relation of thought or experience to that reality.[10] In expressing his view the anti-realist therefore does best to say: 'Anti-realism is the thesis that, with respect to a given domain, any full description of the objects of thought or experience in that domain has to make essential reference to the thinker or experiencer and the conditions under which the thinking or experience occurs.'

And this is the least that Berkeley means by 'within the mind'. Of course, it is clear that Berkeley is not only an anti-realist but also an idealist, and that the latter, metaphysical thesis depends crucially on his argument for the former, epistemological thesis. The fact that anti-realism and idealism are independent theses (one can be committed to either without being committed to the other) is masked in Berkeley's case by the fact that his 'in the mind' idiom does duty both for 'with essential reference to mind' and 'made of mind-stuff'. But it is not hard to know which reading is intended at any point in his exposition.

Equipped with this account of Berkeley's commitments and method, we can restate his argument as follows. If we examine the phenomenology of consciousness (level 1) we see that it consists of sensory data, notions and compounds

---

10 I argue this at greater length in *An Introduction to Philosophical Logic*, Blackwell, 1997, pp. 310–12.

of either or both of these. Experience is generally orderly, giving rise to the familiar phenomena of level 2 – apples and trees, stones and books (P1). We are also intimately acquainted with ourselves as the subjects of this experience, and not merely as passive recipients of it but causally active participants who will, imagine and remember (P2). Nothing of level 1 can be conceived without reference to the minds for which they exist as the contents of consciousness. But because the phenomena of level 2 are constituted by data of level 1, neither therefore can the phenomena of level 2 be conceived independently of the minds for which they are phenomena (P3). It is commonly held that sensible objects exist independently of mind; but this, on the foregoing, is a contradiction which rests on the mistaken doctrine of abstraction (P4, 5). It follows that the only substance there can be is mind or spirit (P6, 7).

The argument has made no explicit mention of material substance; the first full-dress appearance of matter, as the focus of 'received opinion' in this debate, has to wait a further ten paragraphs (P16–17). But the denial of its possibility has already been registered, for if things are ideas, and ideas are essentially mental, then nothing other than mind can substantiate them. The doctrine that there is 'unthinking stuff' which is the substance of things *qua* collections of ideas is accordingly an obvious 'repugnancy' (contradiction): for how can an unthinking thing have ideas? (P7).

A crucial consideration for Berkeley in rejecting the

concept of material substance is that there are no empirical grounds for it; its philosophical supporters (he has Locke in mind) 'acknowledge they have no other meaning annexed to those sounds, but the idea of being in general, together with the relative notion of its supporting accidents' (P17). Berkeley finds the concept of 'being in general' the most 'abstract and incomprehensible' he has ever encountered, and he has no time for the metaphor of 'support' invoked to explain the relation between matter and its accidents. But more importantly still, the only thing which we are entitled to say is causally efficacious is spirit or mind (P26–7); ideas are the effects of the causal activity of mind, whether our own or that of an infinite spirit (P28–33).

In the course of unfolding his argument, Berkeley tells us that although there is a distinction between primary and secondary qualities, they are the same in one crucial respect: they are both *sensible* properties, and therefore cannot exist otherwise than as ideas, and therefore again cannot exist otherwise than in relation to mind (P9–15). He also points out that since nothing but an idea can be like an idea, the seductive thought that ideas are resemblances or copies which represent non-ideas makes no sense: can we, he asks, 'assert that a colour is like something which is invisible; hard or soft, like something which is intangible; and so of the rest'? (P8).

A key concept in the foregoing is that of ideas. Berkeley uses 'idea' to mean 'any immediate object of sense or understanding', but as already noted he is careful to distinguish this from what, in the second paragraph of P, he had described as 'such as are perceived by attending to the passions and operations of the mind', which he later calls *notions*. The distinction is as follows. Ideas are always *sensory*; they are either the content of states of sensory awareness, or the copies of these in memory and imagination. *Notions* on the other hand are concepts of spirit – of self, mind and God – and have a more complex origin. As regards self-knowledge, notions originate in immediate intuition; as regards other minds, in interpretation; and as regards God, in 'reflexion and reasoning' (P42, 140–2, 3D232).

Two features of ideas are crucial for Berkeley: their *inertness* and their *mind-dependence*. They are the latter simply in virtue of being ideas. Their being the former is a more intricate matter. Anticipating Hume, Berkeley argues that there are no necessary connections between ideas; they are individual entities 'with no power or agency included in them. So that one idea or object of thought cannot produce or make an alteration in another' (P25). We verify this by introspecting, which reveals, says Berkeley, that 'there is nothing in [ideas] but what we perceive', and we perceive no power or activity in them (P25). We have a 'continual succession' of ideas, some arising and others disappearing; but because they are causally inert, they are not themselves responsible for these changes, so there must be some other cause of them (P26). The only candidate remaining for this role is spirit or mind. Since my mind is causally responsible for very few ideas and their changes, there must be 'some other spirit that produces them' (P29).

Berkeley gives the name *perception* to any way of having ideas and notions before the mind, in sensing, conceiving, imagining, remembering, reasoning and the rest. It is accordingly a generic term, and is not restricted to sensory perception alone. 'Perceiving' denotes a causal relation: minds perceive ideas either by causing them (as when finite minds imagine or dream, and as when the infinite mind wills the existence of the universe) or by being causally affected by them (as when finite minds receive the ideas caused by God, = encounter the physical world).

Any inference to the nature of the spirit that is causally responsible for ideas and their changes must start from the nature of those ideas and their changes. 'The ideas of sense', says Berkeley, again anticipating Hume, 'are more strong, lively, and distinct than those of imagination; they have likewise a steadiness, order, and coherence, and are not excited at random, as those which are the effects of human wills often are, but in a regular train or series' (P30). These 'set rules or methods' we call *'Laws of Nature*; and these we learn by experience, which teaches us that such and such ideas are attended with such and such other ideas, in the ordinary course of things' (P30). From this Berkeley concludes that God, the 'Author of Nature', is the ultimate source of ideas and their connections.

From this in turn it follows that although everything that exists is mind-dependent, it is not dependent on particular or finite minds, but has an objective source and structure, namely, the eternal, ubiquitous and law-like perceiving of an infinite mind. This is the sense in which Berkeley is a realist; the world exists independently of the thought and experience of finite minds (2D166–7) – which explains what he means by claiming to defend common sense, for common sense holds that grass is green and the sky is blue whether or not any of us happen to be looking at either, whereas Locke and the corpuscularians held otherwise – grass has powers to make us see green, but it is not itself green; indeed, on the Lockean view the world is colourless, odourless and silent until perceived, when it produces in the perceiver visual, olfactory and auditory experiences. But for Berkeley the world is just as we perceive it to be even when we are not perceiving it, because it is always and everywhere perceived by the infinite mind of a deity.

The deity perceives the universe by thinking it; that is, causing it to exist by conceiving it. In a letter to the American Dr Samuel Johnson, Berkeley remarks that his view differs only verbally from the theological doctrine that God maintains the universe in existence by an act of continual creation. So the ideas which constitute the world are caused by the deity, and appear in our consciousnesses as the effects of his causal activity: this is the *metaphysical* way (level 3) of describing what, in ordinary terminology, we describe as seeing trees, tasting ice-cream, and so forth. The latter way of describing the facts is not incorrect; Berkeley's argument is that the ordinary and the metaphysical ways of describing reality are alternative descriptions of the same thing.

A significant feature of this account is its view of causality. Locke had argued that the empirical basis for our concept of causality comes from our own felt powers as agents, able to initiate and intervene in trains of events in the world. This sense of our own efficacy we 'project' onto the world to explain chains of events in it, imputing to events we describe as 'causes' an agency or power on analogy with our own. For Berkeley the projective move is empirically ungrounded. We indeed have experience of causal agency as spirits, which are the only active things we know. But although it is a convenience to impute causal agency to things (ideas) in our ordinary way of talking, they are inert, and apparent causal connections between them are ultimately owed to the regular, consistent, lawlike causal activity of God.

It is obvious that Berkeley's theory rests upon a vital and very debatable assumption, borrowed unquestioningly from Locke who equally unquestioningly borrowed it from the Cartesians; namely, that the place to begin philosophical enquiry is among the private data of individual consciousness – that is, among the ideas constituting an individual's experience. If one accepts this Cartesian super-premise (a large 'If'), the early steps of Berkeley's argument appear persuasive, as may be seen by considering a proposed objection

24

to it; namely, that it commits the elementary error of identifying sensible qualities and sensory ideas. For – says the objection – there is a large difference between 'The table is brown' and 'The table looks brown to me', because the truth-conditions of the two statements differ. The table could be brown without it seeming so to me, and vice versa; so Berkeley's argument collapses.

But this argument begs the question against Berkeley by assuming that claims about what qualities an object possesses are independent of claims about how they can be known to possess them; which amounts to the claim that there are observation-independent facts about the qualities of objects which can be stated without any reference to experience of them. But this claim is exactly what Berkeley rejects, on the grounds that any characterization of a sensible quality has to make essential reference to how it appears to some actual or possible perceiver. How, he asks, does one explain redness, smoothness and other sensible qualities independently of how they appear? So the objection fails by premising a seems–is distinction which is precisely what Berkeley opposes on the grounds that it leads to scepticism.

To deny that there is a seems–is distinction is just another way of asserting that sensible objects (things in the world) are collections of sensible qualities, and hence of ideas. So Berkeley takes the contrast he wishes to resist to be one between (a) sensible objects, which as collections of sensible qualities are what is immediately perceived, and (b) objects existing independently of perception but causing it. This is not the same contrast as (c) sense data in the sense of un-interpreted contents of sensory states, and (a) sensible objects. It is important to note this because for Berkeley what is immediately present in experience is the sensible object, not some mediating representation (or collection of representations) different from the object. We do not, he says, infer from colour patches and other sensory data to the existence, in a world beyond them, of books and trees; what we see (and touch etc.) are, immediately, books and trees.

This, however, prompts another objection, this time that Berkeley is having things both ways: he says that we immediately perceive such familiar objects of sense-experience as books and trees, while at the same time saying that what we immediately perceive are colours and textures. To see what is involved here, consider an argument advanced in more recent philosophy. This says that books and trees are interpretations of, or inferences from, the sensory data of experience, and that in speaking of books rather than colour patches we are going beyond what talk of colour patches strictly licenses. This is because we take physical objects to exist independently of particular perceivings of them, to be publicly available to more than one perceiver at a time, and so on – none of which is true of the sensory ideas from which they are inferred. So we have to keep (a) and (c) strictly separate.

Berkeley can be defended against this objection by appealing to the distinction of levels. At level 1 we immediately perceive colours and textures, while at level 2 we immediately perceive books and trees. The latter consist wholly of the former, and it is only if one disregards the distinction of levels that one might fall into the mistake of thinking that when one perceives a smooth red book, one perceives redness and smoothness *and* a book, as if the book were something additional to the sensible qualities constituting it. Just such a view is forced by the materialist view, in which something inaccessible to sensory awareness constitutes the underlying causal origin of the sensible qualities we perceive.

Some critics object that having thus argued that all perception is immediate, Berkeley promptly proceeds to admit a species of *mediate* perception by inference or 'suggestion'. The passage cited is the one where Berkeley says, 'When I hear a coach drive along the streets, immediately I perceive only the sound; but from the experience I have had that such a sound is connected with a coach, I am said to hear the coach' (1D204). This might count as a case of mediate perception if Berkeley did not immediately add, 'It is nevertheless evident, that in truth and strictness, nothing can be *heard* but *sound*: and the coach is not then properly perceived by sense, but suggested from experience.' The same applies to our practice of saying elliptically that one sees that the poker is hot; again, one does not see heat, one sees *that* something is hot; that is, one infers on the basis of experience that when something looks like that, it will feel a certain way if you

27

touch it. These are not cases of mediate perception, but of experience-based inference, to which Berkeley gives the name 'suggestion': the ideas of one sense *suggest* the ideas of another.

The foregoing shows that as long as certain of Berkeley's premises are accepted, and as long as discussion of the main plank of his views (the notion of God and his metaphysical activity) is deferred, his views are resilient to objection. If we reject the Cartesian super-premise – that the place to start is the data of individual experience – his views are not nearly so resilient.[11]

These remarks touch upon one set of objections to Berkeley's views. Others, as remarked, more threatening to his position, concern its underpinning; namely, the infinite mind to which a central metaphysical role is allotted. This is discussed below.

---

11 But it must be said, in relation to this strategy, that in adopting such an approach one is well advised to keep sight of the subjective perspective, for any account of the nature of experience and its relation to knowledge has to be sensitive to the fact – for fact it is – that each subject of experience is to some degree in the solipsistic and finitary predicament which the Cartesian tradition emphasizes. This remains so even if we argue, as we doubtless should, that assumptions about shared language and therefore a shared world, on which we have a participant rather than a merely passive perspective, provide material for a better account.

The concept of matter is redundant, Berkeley's argument purports to demonstrate, because everything required to explain the world and experience of it is available in recognizing that minds and ideas are all there can be. But Berkeley adds to this argument-by-exclusion a set of positive antimaterialist considerations.

An important argument for materialism is that use of a concept of matter explains much in science. Berkeley summarizes the view thus:

> There have been a great many things explained by matter and motion: take away these, and you destroy the whole corpuscular philosophy, and undermine those mechanical principles which have been applied with such success to account for the phenomena. In short, whatever advances have been made . . . in the study of nature, do all proceed on the supposition that corporeal substance or matter doth really exist. (P50)

Berkeley's reply is that science's explanatory power and practical utility neither entail the truth of, nor depend upon, the materialist hypothesis, for these can equally, if not better (because more economically) be explained in instrumentalist terms. Instrumentalism is the view that scientific theories are tools, and as such are not candidates for assessment as true or false, but rather as more or less useful. One does not ask whether a gardening utensil such as a spade is true, but whether it does its intended job effectively – and not merely effectively, but, as required by Ockham's Razor, as simply and economically as possible.

Berkeley expressed his early version of instrumentalism as a 'doctrine of signs', in which the regularity and order among our ideas reflect the steady will of God, which is so reliable that we can represent the connections thus observed as laws. He writes, 'The steady, consistent methods of Nature, may not unfitly be styled the *language* of its Author, whereby he . . . directs us how to act for the convenience and felicity of life' (P109). Science is thus a convenient summary, for sublunary purposes, of what at the metaphysical level of explanation would be described in terms of the activity of infinite spirit.

This is a rejoinder to an attempted 'appeal to the best explanation' on behalf of the materialist hypothesis. It is at the same time a rejoinder to a closely allied argument, an 'appeal to the simplest explanation'. This says that postulating the existence of matter simplifies the account we give of the world. The rejoinder consists in the same slash of Ockham's Razor; it is that since experience could be exactly as it is without matter existing independently of it, the materialist hypothesis is not the simplest explanation after all.

But the key point for Berkeley is that whatever else matter is, by definition (a) it is non-mental, and as such cannot be the support of qualities, because qualities are ideas, and ideas can only exist in a thinking substance; and (b) it is inert, that is, causally inactive, and so cannot produce change, motion or ideas.

For Locke and others among Berkeley's predecessors the concept of primary qualities was important because, they held, experience of them puts us most closely in touch with independent reality. Berkeley rejects their view on the ground, already mentioned, that 'nothing can be like an idea but an idea' (P8). Materialists hold that primary qualities are 'resemblances' of 'things which exist without the mind' (P9); but since primary qualities are ideas, and only ideas can resemble ideas, it follows that 'neither they nor their archetypes can be in an unperceiving substance' (P9). Moreover, as also already noted, the primary–secondary quality distinction, understood in terms of a supposed difference between the way each kind of quality relates to mind, involves a specious abstraction of one kind from the other; for since one cannot conceive such primary qualities as motion or number apart from such secondary qualities as colour, both are on a par in the way they relate to mind, viz. by being essentially dependent upon mind for their existence as ideas.

Some of Berkeley's critics think he failed to separate the question of material substance from that of the primary–secondary quality distinction, since one can reject materialism while retaining the distinction. But this in fact is what Berkeley does, for he does not deny that there is a distinction between primary and secondary qualities – he recognizes that the former are available to more than one sense at a time, the latter available to one sense only; that the former are measurable, the latter not (or not so straightforwardly); and so on – but he points out that in the *crucial* respect of their relation to mind, they are on a par in both being *sensible* and hence mind-dependent.

One charge levelled at Berkeley is that his account of the crucial relation between minds and ideas is contradictory or at very least confused. At P2 he says that the mind 'is a thing *entirely distinct* from [ideas], *wherein they exist*, or, which is the same thing, whereby they are perceived' (my emphases). At P5 he adds that it is not possible to conceive 'any sensible thing or object *distinct from* the sensation or perception of it', and in the same paragraph he remarks, 'Is it possible to separate, even in thought, my ideas from perception? For my part, I might as easily divide a thing from itself.' These assertions appear to commit him to three principles which are together inconsistent, but which each play an important part in his argument.[12]

---

12 This question has additional importance in that resolving it in the way I here propose contributes to settling a debate which has much exercised Berkeley scholars in recent decades: Edwin Allaire's 'inherence pattern' argument, proposing that Berkeley's view is that since mind is the substance of the world, the relation that ideas bear to mind is that of inherence, and that 'perceives' is explicated by 'inheres in'. See Robert G. Muehlmann, *Berkeley's Metaphysics*, Pennsylvania State University Press, 1995, esp. the Introduction and essays in Part I *passim*.

The three principles have been called the *Distinction Principle*, asserting that minds and ideas are distinct from one another (P2, 27, 80, 142); the *Inherence Principle*, asserting that ideas exist only in the mind (P2, 3 and *passim*); and the *Identity Principle*, asserting that ideas are not distinct from perceivings of them (P5, 1D195 ff.). The second and third are consistent; the first and third appear to contradict each other; and the relation between the first two at very least demands explanation.

Most critics think that the best solution is to abandon the Distinction Principle. One reason is that it appears to commit Berkeley to an *act–object* analysis of perception, whereas the Identity Principle commits him to an *adverbial* analysis. The first describes perceiving as an act of mind directed upon an object, rather as the beam of a torch is directed upon something we wish to illuminate: the object is independent of the act, which can be repeated with different objects (the act of looking, like the beam of the torch, can have as its successive objects a book, a cat, a desk). The adverbial analysis has it that perception is a modification of the mind, so that, for example, to see a cat is to have one's mind shaped or modified into a 'catly-perceiving state'. Here there is one event – the modification of one's mental states in a certain way – whereas on the act–object analysis there is the mental act and something independent of it, *viz.* its object. Since this analysis demands the *independence* of the objects of perception, which on Berkeley's theory are ideas and hence incapable of independence from mind, the Distinction Principle seems to be the obvious candidate for rejection.

But the principle is crucial to Berkeley; the very plan of P depends on it: 'Human knowledge [reduces] to two heads, that of *ideas* and that of *spirits*' (P86). And this is no surprise, since if the principle were rejected, minds would be identical with their ideas; but this cannot be, for Berkeley insists on the differences: minds are active, ideas inert; ideas are dependent entities, minds substantial. In C Berkeley had considered and rejected the notion (yet again anticipating Hume) that minds are just bundles of ideas, on the good ground that 'a colour cannot perceive a sound, nor a sound a colour . . . therefore I am one individual principle, distinct from colour and sound; and, for the same reason, from all other sensible things and inert ideas' (3D234).

The Distinction Principle therefore cannot be abandoned. But neither can the others; the Inherence Principle, after all, is simply a version of *esse est percipi*, and the Identity Principle follows from the attack on abstraction, which tells us that we cannot abstract ideas from perception of them. Is there a solution?

There is, and it is to be found in recognizing that the expressions 'Inherence' and 'Identity' are misleading. For Berkeley does not hold that ideas 'inhere' in the mind, as attributes are said to inhere in substance, nor that ideas and perception of them are identical. I take each point in turn.

The Inherence Principle states that 'ideas exist in the mind'. The formula 'in the mind', as already noted, is to be understood as 'with essential reference to mind', in the sense that the existence of an idea is dependent upon its being perceived – *actually*, not just *possibly*, perceived: recall that in Berkeley's theory everything that exists is actual. The sense of 'dependence' here is that in which (to adapt an obstetric example of Plato's) an embryo is dependent on a womb: it exists in it, and cannot exist without it, but it is nevertheless distinct from it. 'Inherence' is an adverbial notion, whereas Berkeley holds that ideas and minds stand in the internal causal relation denoted by the generic concept of perception: 'There can be no substratum of . . . qualities but spirit, in which they exist, not by way of mode or property, but as a thing perceived in that which perceives it' (3D237).

As for the Identity Principle, it is a straightforward mistake to construe Berkeley's anti-abstractionist view – namely, that any account of ideas cannot be abstracted from an account of perception – as amounting to an assertion of the identity of ideas with perception of them. The assertion that one cannot 'conceive apart' any 'sensible thing or object distinct from the perception of it' (P5) is not a claim that these are numerically the same thing. Consider an example: bread and the process by which it is baked are internally related; there cannot be one without the other; but bread is not numerically identical with the baking of it. The same kind of internality characterizes the relation of minds and ideas. As one would expect, that merely iterates the point made about the Inherence Principle.

The question of the mind–idea relation is important because it is the only major threat to the *internal* coherence of Berkeley's theory. These comments show that there is not after all such a threat. As before, it remains that the Cartesian basis of the project, and its linchpin metaphysical thesis that an infinite mind perceives everything always, are the two real problems with Berkeley's theory. It is time to consider the second of these.

Berkeley took his arguments to amount to a new and powerful argument for the existence of a God. As such, as noted, they are a contribution to natural theology; nothing turns on revelation or traditional conceptions of deity, beyond that such a being has to be infinite and omnipotent. Indeed, Berkeley's arguments require no more than a metaphysical God thus conceived. Whether such a being is a person, or whether it is interested in what it has created, is neither here nor there, so long as it fulfils its function of making the universe exist.

The nub of Berkeley's argument for God is that since everything that exists is either mind or ideas, and since finite minds, even in concert, could not perceive all the ideas that constitute the universe, there must be an infinite mind which perceives everything always and thereby keeps it in being.

The classic statement of the argument occurs in the second of the *Three Dialogues* (2D212–14). From the proposition 'that sensible things cannot exist otherwise than in a mind or spirit' Berkeley concludes, 'Not that they have no real existence, but that seeing they depend not on my thought, and have an existence distinct from being perceived by me, *there must be some other mind wherein they exist.*' This conclusion is a weaker one than that there is a single infinite mind which perceives everything always; it establishes no more than that there is 'some other mind' – who might, for all we know, be the next-door neighbour. But in the very next sentence Berkeley adds, 'As sure therefore as the sensible world really exists, so sure is there an infinite omnipresent spirit who contains and supports it.' This is quite a leap. The missing step is provided later (2D215):

I perceive numberless ideas; and by an act of my Will can form a great variety of them, and raise them up in my imagination: though it must be confessed, these creatures of the fancy are not altogether so distinct, so strong, vivid, permanent, as those perceived by my senses, which latter are called *real things*. From all which I conclude, *there is a mind which affects me every moment with all the sensible impressions I perceive.* And from the variety, order and manner of these, I conclude the Author of them to be *wise, powerful, and good beyond comprehension.*' This 'Author' Berkeley a few lines later describes as 'God the Supreme and Universal Cause of all things.

The missing step is, accordingly, a version of the teleological argument for the existence of a God.

The argument in fact has two stages. The first argues that things are causally dependent on mind for their existence, and therefore, since I cannot think of everything always, there must be mental activity elsewhere carrying out the task. The second stage says that one can infer the character of that mind by inspecting the nature of its ideas: since the universe is so huge, beautiful, intricate and so on, it must be a '*wise, powerful*' and so on, mind.

The first thing to note is the inadequacy of the teleological argument here co-opted as the second stage. The appearance of design, purpose or beauty in the universe does not entail that it was designed; and even if it did entail this, it does not thereby entail that it was designed by a single mind, or an infinite mind, or a good mind. (What if – regarding this last point – we reflected on the cruelty in nature, and the disease, waste, pain and other evils abundant there? What picture of a creating mind would this suggest?) In any case there are more economical ways to explain the teleological appearance of the universe, the best being evolutionary theory.

What of the first stage? The most it establishes is the conclusion that what exists can do so only in relation to mind. The relation in question needs to be explained; Berkeley is committed to saying that it is a *causal* relation, but it is exactly this which pushes him to the unpersuasive second stage of the argument for an infinite mind. An alternative resource might be to say that there is no account to be given of the world which does not make essential reference to facts about thought or experience of it, and this might furnish the starting point for views like Kant's or those of certain contemporary 'anti-realists'.

Although Berkeley does not need the God of traditional theology but only a metaphysical being causally competent for its task, his employment of teleological considerations mixes tradition with metaphysics to the injury of the latter. There is certainly no shadow of an argument why the mental activity to which the existence of the whole universe is referred has to be a single mind or an infinite one. A committee of finite minds might seem an even less palatable option, but nothing in the argument excludes it.

Upon inspection, accordingly, the argument for the metaphysical linchpin of Berkeley's theory does not work. As remarked, if this does not entail the collapse of the project, it will be because there is some other way of substantiating the idea that what exists stands in an internal relation to thought or experience of it. On that score, philosophy is not without resources.

Other points in Berkeley's views repay further examination, for example his concept of conceivability, his finitary realism, the character of his idealism, his views of time, and – as just suggested – the metaphysical implications of his arguments considered independently of their theistic basis. I discuss these at length in my *Berkeley: The Central Arguments*

(Duckworth, 1986). But enough has been said to suggest reasons for his influence on later thinkers, not least among them the Phenomenalists and the Logical Positivists. It is in particular both interesting and philosophically important to understand why phenomenalism, as a version of Berkeley's theory in which the bare concept of 'possibilities of perception' ('possibilia') has been substituted for the concept of a deity, is arguably less cogent than the original. From the point of view of acceptability there is little to choose between a metaphysics of possibilia and a theological basis for the universe, neither of which is anywhere near attractive. But at least in Berkeley's thesis, everything that exists is actual.

CHAPTER 2

Russell, Experience and the Roots of Science

Empiricism is the family of theories which in one or another way locate the source or at very least the test of contingent knowledge in experience – specifically, in sensory experience. More circumstantially: it is the family of theories which variously require experiential grounds for concepts to have content or applicability, or for expressions in a given language to have sense. In these versions of a formulation, due allowance is made for the thought that the content of perceptual states, suitably construed, are to be considered the occasion or basis for certain kinds of fundamental judgements from which, together with other premises, our less fundamental judgements about the world (or things other than the content of those states of sensitivity themselves) can be inferred.

In a qualified sense of this broadly characterized position, Russell was an empiricist, and his epistemology remained in that qualified sense empiricist throughout its development. But he was also critical of certain forms of empiricism, and the focus of his own concerns were such that his aims in

41

formulating epistemological views, and his evolving attempts to realize these aims in detail, are not straightforwardly traditional. The chief reason for this is that his overarching concern was the question of how science is related to subjective experience, beginning (in the work done in 1911–14) with attempts to show how the fundamental concepts of physics can be derived from experience, and ending (in 1948) by shifting attention to the question of the non-empirical features of knowledge-acquisition required for bridging the gap between experience and science.

In these aims for epistemology Russell was remarkably consistent throughout the period 1911–48, which is to say, from the time he finished work on the first edition of PM[1] until his last major philosophical book, HK. His concern was not the traditional epistemological one of showing that knowledge is justified by experience, where this task is typically specified by a response to sceptical arguments. Russell was thoroughly Lockean in his attitude to the theory of knowledge, in the

---

1 The standard abbreviations of Russell's works are employed throughout: PM = *Principia Mathematica*, PoM = *Principles of Mathematics*, HK = *Human Knowledge: Its Scope and Limits*, PP = *Problems of Philosophy*, TK = *Theory of Knowledge*, OKEW = *Our Knowledge of the External World*, ML = *Mysticism and Logic*, LK = *Logic and Knowledge* (ed. Marsh), AMi = *Analysis of Mind*, AMt = *Analysis of Matter*, IMT = *Inquiry into Meaning and Truth*, PE = *Philosophical Essays*.

sense that he did not think scepticism a serious option, and therefore did not waste time attempting to rebut it. Rather, he conceived epistemology's proper task as one of displaying how one gets from sense experience to science. For Russell this was an explanatory, not a justificatory, task.

In the cluster of texts addressing the question of the experience–science relation in the immediate post-PM period, Russell describes his aim as showing how physics is 'verified' by observation and experiment – by which he meant: having its predictions confirmed by these means. Given that all that can be directly observed are the data of sense, he saw the question as one of explaining the correlation of the contents of the physical world with the data of sensory experience by which they are alone verifiable.[2] He did not put the point by saying that *claims* about the content of the physical world are verified (still less justified) by sensory experience; and this is neither an accidental nor a merely historically conditioned trick of formulation. It is a feature of robust realism not to construe the point of epistemology as being the justification of knowledge-claims, but as being an explication of the relation between what the claims are about and the nature of experience. 'Justifying science by grounding it in experience' and 'showing how physics succeeds in being an empirical science, based on observation and experiment' are two different aims, and Russell's was the latter.

2   'The Relation of Sense-Data to Physics', ML p. 145.

In PP, which gives the outlines of Russell's early view in popular form, the project begins by adopting the Cartesian air of a justificatory, scepticism-rebutting enterprise. The same is true of the discussion in IMT and Russell's replies in Schilpp. But that was because Russell saw the principal task of showing how experience and science relate as the obverse of the coin whose reverse is the more familiar form of discussion in which experience is invoked as the ground of knowledge. Because Russell assumed throughout that science is (or at least is on the way to discovering) the truth about the world (and his considered views consistently respected this assumption), he did not see epistemology's task to be the defence of science against doubt, but instead to be the demonstration of how finite human subjectivity acquires knowledge of the objective reality which science describes. In showing this, it also shows that the degree of certainty possible in contingent knowledge is less than absolute. In this sense, Russell was happy to concede something to scepticism without being much troubled by it; after all – so in effect he thought – what else is to be expected from contingent empirical knowledge?

In the earlier phases of his endeavour Russell saw the task of technical philosophy (philosophy conceived as logic; in fact, though, this aspect of Russell's endeavour is more accurately described as metaphysics) as principally being one of showing how the fundamental concepts of science (as he then took them to be) – space, time, causality and matter – can be constructed, and in his view this was a more important and more interesting matter than the epistemological question of how one relatively insignificant fragment of reality – humanity – manages more or less successfully to represent the rest of reality to itself. It is easy to overlook the fact that these two of Russell's tasks – the logical construction of the then-conceived fundamental scientific concepts, and the question of how finite subjective experience connects with scientific knowledge – are different, although of course they impinge upon one another at most points. But Russell's attention came rapidly to focus almost exclusively on the epistemological task, to which the larger part of his strictly philosophical writings after 1911 were addressed.

What changed over time in Russell's thought after 1911 was not his epistemological aim, but the strategies he successively adopted to try to achieve it. Perhaps because science itself dramatically altered the question of which concepts are fundamental to it (space and time had become space–time in Einstein's theories, and matter had vanished in the wake of both of them and quantum theory), Russell ceased to look for a logical construction of these specific concepts. Indeed, he abandoned the logical constructivist programme long before the likes of Carnap and Goodman attempted them, and before Wisdom had shown that getting the world out of sense-data without residue is impossible.[3]

---

3   See R. Carnap, 'Logical Construction of the World', N. Goodman, 'The Structure of Appearance', Wisdom J. *Mind*, 1932–4.

The continuities and developments in Russell's relation-of-sense-to-science project are well displayed as the similarities and contrasts between his description of the project's aims, and of the methods to be employed in carrying it out, in the 1911–14 writings and HK in 1948. Commentators generally take at face value Russell's own claim, in MPD, that in AMi (1921) he abandoned not just the nomenclature of the sense-datum theory but what it was trying to achieve; and this is taken, among other things, to mark a more expressly 'neutral monist' turn as the metaphysical basis of his epistemological efforts until, in his very late work, another and final shift of perspective occurs, this time away from efforts to carry out the original project and towards the task of identifying the non-empirical supplements which, by that stage, he saw as the chief interest in discussing the bridge over the experience–science gap. But in fact it can be shown that despite the asseverations of MPD and the apparent elimination of the subject in AMi (courtesy of Russell's by then further developed conception of the 'neutral monist' stance), the underlying theme of specifying the connections between experience and science remained. Of course, from the period of AMi onward Russell changed the terms of the relation at issue dramatically; acquaintance vanished, and was replaced (to begin with) by 'noticing' (experiential salience) and successor conceptions. Acquaintance and the subject seemed to go so intimately together that their departure appeared jointly necessary; but it is no surprise to find the epistemic subject still in view in HK, having been merely in disguise in the interim.

The purpose in what follows is accordingly to illustrate, by way of an account of the development of Russell's project, the remarkable consistency of aim it displays. I do this by tracing the project's history, chiefly to establish an accurate characterization of it, but also to provide a corrective to the impression that in epistemology Russell merely offered a sequence of *ad hoc* moves in response to a problem which has since been understood, but even then was already beginning to be recognized, as misconceived, *viz.* the endeavour to erect a justificatory theory of knowledge on the flawed Cartesian grounds of deriving certainty from the private data of experience. But to repeat: Russell's task was, significantly, different from that; he wished not to see epistemology as a justificatory enterprise aimed at refuting scepticism, but as a descriptive enterprise aimed at explaining the fact (which he did not question) that finite subjects attain scientific knowledge. He was thus a naturalist long before Quine or anyone else, despite Cartesianly not insisting, as later naturalists did, that one cannot premise science in epistemology.[4] And he was therefore far more consistent in his aims and principles than most (agreeing with Charles Broad) have allowed.

4   See TK pp. 50–2. See also A. C. Grayling, 'Naturalistic Assumptions', later in this volume.

Certain corollaries attend the picture I offer. One is that Hylton misdescribes Russell's turn to epistemological themes after PM as involving 'considerable concessions to psychologism'.[5] Whatever else the label means, 'psychologism' is at least the view that the objects of acquaintance and judgement (to use period Russellian terms for the purpose) cannot themselves be described independently of features attaching to them as a result of the psychological conditions of their apprehension. This is never Russell's claim, and indeed anything like it was expressly disavowed in his pre-PoM flight from idealism.[6] Post-PM Russell was realist to excess, rather than psychologistic, in allowing a wider range of objective targets of acquaintance than a traditional empiricist would allow, embracing as it did both physical particulars and abstract entities of various kinds. So much is familiar. And this is not to deny that Russell's interests lay in connecting the content of psychological states (mental states of the subject-relatum in acquaintance and judgement) with the independent objects such states brought into the subject's ken; for, after all, it was the 'transition from sense to science' as he still called it at the end of his philosophical life (MPD 153) that was his focus, and this requires addressing the question of what and how much the psychological states of epistemic

---

5   P. Hylton, *Russell, Idealism, and the Emergence of Analytic Philosophy*, Oxford University Press, 1990, p. 330.
6   See, for example ML p. 101.

subjects can be said to give them of objective scientific truth.

A corollary of the consistency thesis which I here argue on Russell's behalf is that the celebrated derailment of Russell's project in TK, ascribed to Wittgenstein as a result of some (characteristically hyperbolic) remarks by Russell in a letter to Lady Ottoline Morrell, might not be quite what it seems; for in a footnote added to the text of 'On Knowledge by Acquaintance and Knowledge by Description' when this 1911 essay was reprinted in ML in 1917, Russell remarks of his multiple relation theory of judgement, 'I have been persuaded by Mr Wittgenstein that this theory is somewhat unduly simple, but the modification which I believe it to require does not affect [its fundamentals].' The same point occurs more fully in LLA[7] where Russell discusses the difficulties faced by the theory, involving subordinate 'verbs'. He subsequently, somewhat without fanfare, abandoned the theory; but it is clear from the fact that he continued to the end with the larger project of clarifying the experience–science connection that he found his multiple relation theory of judgement to be inessential to it; and therefore the fact that Russell dismembered TK and left some parts of it unused is not the same as his abandoning the project in whose working out TK was a chapter.

A good way to begin is to observe the images Russell employs early and late in preparing readers for the epistemo-

---

7   Lectures on Logical Atomism, 1918.

logical task as he conceived it. In the Preface to HK he observes that the terms 'belief', 'truth', 'knowledge' and 'perception' all have imprecise common uses which will require progressive clarification as the enquiry proceeds. 'Our increase of knowledge, assuming that we are successful, is like that of a traveller approaching a mountain through a haze: at first only certain large features are discernible, and even they have indistinct boundaries, but gradually more detail becomes visible and edges become sharper.' Compare this to what Russell says in TK of the ambiguities of the words 'experience', 'mind', 'knowledge' and 'perception': 'The meanings of common words are vague, fluctuating and ambiguous, like the shadow thrown by a flickering street-lamp on a windy night; yet in the nucleus of this uncertain patch of meaning, we may find some precise concept for which philosophy requires a name' – which, Russell concludes, should best be the common expressions themselves, made suitably definite. Imagery aside, part of the method of both early and late epistemology is thus characterized as the same: clarification of concepts, on one familiar view the central task of analysis characteristic of 'analytic philosophy'. But Russell also took the view that analysis is only the propaedeutical part of the story; more important (so he early believed and hoped) was the constructive task of showing how complexes of various kinds – and not least, knowledge of complexes – can be constructed out of simples: early on, the simples with which we are acquainted. The constructive task is the one which ended in failure, and the changes in Russell's epistemology are a direct function of the difficulties met with in the course of the project, which he increasingly saw as insurmountable. The hope had been to couple analysis and synthesis, the first activity preparing the way for the second, reflecting Russell's early ambition, formed on a walk one day in Berlin in the 1890s, to link abstract and scientific knowledge into a grand synthesis.

The synthetic task failed, but one thing which did not change was the aim subserved by the method developed to carry it out. In TK Russell plunges straight into the task of analysing acquaintance, which he calls 'the simplest and most pervading aspect of experience', a dyadic relation (an important point, for cognate polyadic relations of higher order constitute something significantly different, namely, judgements) between a 'mental subject' and what turn out to be the catholically conceived objects of its attitudes. This was to fulfil a promise implicit in the outline of a programme given in March 1911 in three lectures: the Aristotelian Society address 'Knowledge by Acquaintance and Knowledge by Description', and two lectures delivered in Paris, 'Le Realisme Analytique' and 'L'importance Philosophique de la Logistique'. In the first of these latter he reasserts his commitment to realism both in epistemology and as regards universals, and outlines the technique of analysis of complex into simples to which he there first applies the name 'logical atomism'. In that and the companion lecture he launches the work characteristic of the 1911–14 period, worked out in most detail in a series of papers – 'On Matter' (1912), 'The Relation of Sense-Data to Physics' and 'On Scientific Method in Philosophy' (1914), and 'The Ultimate Constituents of Matter' (1915; the three latter are reprinted in ML) – whose chief precipitate constitutes OKEW (1914).[8] Notoriously, the project was first planned to result in TK; but the difficulties over the theory of judgement obliged Russell to dismantle the task into what he doubtless hoped would be more manageable components.

The project is sketched in a letter from Russell to Ottoline Morrell in October 1912. 'The sort of thing that interests me now is this: some of our knowledge comes from sense, some comes otherwise; what comes otherwise is called "*a priori*". Most actual knowledge is a mixture of both. The analysis of a piece of actual knowledge into pure sense and pure *a priori* is often very difficult, but almost always very important.'[9] Russell had chosen both parts of the task: to trace the transition from sense to science, and to isolate the *a priori* elements of the latter and to axiomatize them, as a preparation for defining the central concepts (space, time, causality and matter itself). Arguably, the epistemological task came to seem press-

---

8   'On Matter' was unpublished until *The Collected Papers of Bertrand Russell*; its dating was ascertained by Kenneth Blackwell from his study of the Russell–Ottoline Morrell correspondence.

9   The letter is dated 30 October 1912.

ing to Russell for the two reasons that whereas, at the outset, the business of defining the fundamental concepts of physics appeared to be a straightforward parallel to defining the fundamental concepts of arithmetic, it quickly transpired that the relation of sense to science was not easy to carry out, and moreover that it was a necessary preliminary to completing the task of logically constructing the concepts of physics from whatever primitive concepts could be discovered in the then fundamental areas of physics, electrodynamics and classical mechanics, together with the relations between them. The reason for the latter is that the empirical content of the primitives requires that they themselves be constructible from sensory experience, as required by the principle that everything we know must be anchored at last in acquaintance.

Russell accordingly deferred the attempt to construct science's central concepts to deal with the epistemological questions first. It is instructive to see how these, in their own right, came to seem to him problematic, given that his first sketch of them (in PP) was an optimistic one, in that it canvassed the traditional questions about the relation of experience to knowledge with a robust acceptance of the fallibility of such knowledge, and the presence in it of assumptions or principles themselves neither independently testable nor matters of logic alone.

In PP Russell introduced the label 'sense-data' to designate what is immediately known in sensation: particular instances in perceptual awareness of colours, sounds, tastes, smells and textures, each class of data corresponding to one of the five sensory modalities. Not only must sense-data be distinguished from acts of sensing them, they must also be distinguished from objects in space outside us with which we suppose them associated. Russell's primary question therefore was: what is the relation of sense-data to these objects?

Russell was not, as noted, concerned to address scepticism. His tack was to say that although sceptical arguments are strictly speaking irrefutable, there is nevertheless 'not the slightest reason' to suppose them true (PP p. 17). Instead he assembles persuasive considerations in support of the view that having sense-data provides access to reasonable knowledge of things in space. First, we can take it that our immediate sensory experiences have a 'primitive certainty'. We recognize that, when we register sense-data which we naturally regard as associated with, say, a table, we have not said everything there is to be said about the table. We think, for example that the table continues to exist when we are not perceiving it, and that the same table is publicly available to more than one perceiver at a time. This makes it clear that a table is something over and above the sense-data that appear to any given subject of experience. But if there were no table existing independently of us in space we should have to formulate a complicated hypothesis about there being as many different seeming-tables as there are perceivers, and explain why nevertheless all the perceivers talk as if they were perceiving the same object.

But note that on the sceptical view, as Russell points out, we ought not even to think that there are other perceivers either, for if we cannot refute scepticism about objects, we are as badly placed to refute scepticism about other minds.

Russell short-circuits the difficulty by accepting a version of the argument to the best explanation. It is simpler and more powerful, he argues, to adopt the hypothesis that, first, there are physical objects existing independently of our sensory experience, and, second, that they cause our perceptions and therefore 'correspond' to them in a reliable way. Following Hume, Russell regards belief in this hypothesis as 'instinctive'.

To this, he argues, we can add another kind of knowledge; namely, *a priori* knowledge of the truths of logic and mathematics. Such knowledge is independent of experience, and depends only on the self-evidence of the truths known. When perceptual knowledge and *a priori* knowledge are conjoined, they enable us to acquire general knowledge of the world beyond immediate experience, for the first kind of knowledge gives us empirical data and the second permits us to draw inferences from it.

These two kinds of knowledge can each be further divided into subkinds, described by Russell as immediate and derivative knowledge respectively. He gives the name 'acquaintance' to immediate knowledge of things. The objects of acquaintance include particulars – that is, individual sense-data (and perhaps ourselves) – and universals. Derivative knowledge of things Russell calls 'knowledge by description', which is general knowledge of facts made possible by combination of and inference from what we are acquainted with.

Immediate knowledge of truths Russell calls 'intuitive knowledge', and he describes the truths so known as *self-evident*. These are propositions which are just 'luminously evident, and not capable of being deduced from anything more evident'. For example, we just *see* that '1 + 1 = 2' is true. Among the items of intuitive knowledge are reports of immediate experience; if I simply state what sense-data I am now aware of, I cannot (barring trivial slips of the tongue) be wrong.

Derivative knowledge of truths consists of whatever can be inferred from self-evident truths by self-evident principles of deduction.

Russell concedes that despite the appearance of rigour introduced by the availability of *a priori* knowledge, we have to accept that ordinary general knowledge is only as good as its foundation in the 'best explanation' justification and the instincts which render it plausible. Ordinary knowledge amounts at best therefore to 'more or less probable opinion'. But when we note that probable opinions form a coherent and mutually supportive system – the more coherent and stable the system, the greater the probability of the opinions forming it – we see why we are entitled to be confident in them.

An important feature of Russell's theory concerns space, and particularly the distinction between the all-embracing public space assumed by science, and the private spaces in which the sense-data of individual perceivers exist. Private space is built out of the various visual, tactual and other experiences which a perceiver co-ordinates into a framework with himself at the centre. But because we do not have acquaintance with the public space of science, its existence and nature is a matter of inference.

Thus Russell's first version of a theory of knowledge, and because its chief outlines are found in PP it is the one most familiarly associated with his name. But he was by no means content with the expression of it in PP, which after all was a popular book and did not essay a rigorous exposition of its theses. The technical papers, TK and OKEW which followed, were his considered versions of these same questions, and mark an advance over this first sketch. One difference between the theories of PP and OKEW is that Russell had come to see that the experiencing subject's basis for knowledge – the sense-data that appear to him alone, and his intuitive knowledge of the laws of logic – is insufficient as a starting point. He accordingly placed greater weight on an experiencer's memories, and his grasp of spatial and temporal relations holding among the elements of occurrent experience. The subject is also empowered to compare data, for example as to differences of colour and shape. Ordinary common beliefs, and belief in the existence of other minds, are still excluded.

This appeal to an enriched conception of cognitive

capacities required at the foundations of knowledge is almost invariably made by empiricist epistemologists – consider Locke and Ayer also – when the thin beams of sensory experience and inference are found, as they invariably are, to be insufficient to bear the weight of knowledge.

With this enriched basis of what he now called 'hard data' Russell reformulated the question to be answered thus: 'Can the existence of anything other than our own hard data be inferred?' His approach was first to show how we can construct, as a hypothesis, a notion of space into which the facts of experience – both the subject's own and those he learns by others' testimony – can be placed. Then, to see whether we have reason for believing that the spatial world is real, Russell gives an argument for believing that other minds exist, because if one is indeed entitled to believe this, then one can rely on the testimony of others, which, jointly with one's own experience, will underwrite the view that there is a spatial (a real) world.

This strategy is ingenious. In 'The Relation of Sense-Data to Physics' Russell adds an equally ingenious way of thinking about the relation of sense-experience to its objects. In PP he had said that we infer the existence of physical things from sense-data; now he described them as functions of or 'constructions' out of sense-data. This employs the technique of logic in which a thing of one (more complex) kind can be shown to be analysable into things of another (simpler) kind. Russell was here relying on what he called the 'supreme maxim of scientific philosophising', namely the principle that 'wherever possible, logical constructions are to be substituted for inferred entities'. Concordantly with this principle, physical objects are to be analysed as constructions out of sense-data – but not out of actual or occurrent sense-data only, but out of possible sense-data too. For actual and possible sense-data Russell coined the term 'sensibilia' by which is meant 'appearances' or, in Russell's phrase, 'how things appear', irrespective of whether they constitute sense-data currently part of any perceiver's experience. This is intended to explain what it is for an object to exist when not being perceived.

An important aspect of this view, Russell now held, is that sensibilia are not private mental entities, but part of the actual subject-matter of physics. They are indeed 'the ultimate constituents of the physical world', because it is in terms of them that verification of common sense and physics ultimately depends. This is important because we usually think that sense-data are functions of physical objects; that is, exist and have their nature because physical objects cause them; but verification is only possible if matters are the other way round, with physical objects as functions of sense-data. This theory 'constructs' physical objects out of sensibilia; the existence of these latter therefore verifies the existence of the former. This view is classically Cartesian.

Such was the epistemology that Russell constructed in the period to 1914. Instead of developing this distinctive theory further, Russell abandoned it. In later work, particularly AMt and HK, he reverted to treating physical objects, and the space they occupy, as inferred from sense-experience. A number of considerations made him do this. One was his acceptance of the standard view offered by physics and physiology that perception is caused by the action of the environment on our sensory surfaces. 'Whoever accepts the causal theory of perception', he wrote (AMt p. 32), 'is compelled to conclude that percepts are in our heads, for they come at the end of a causal chain of physical events leading, spatially, from the object to the brain of the percipient.' In AMi he gave up talk of 'sense-data', and ceased to distinguish between the act of sensing and what is sensed. His reason for this relates to his acceptance – long in coming, for he had repeatedly resisted it in print – of James's 'neutral monism'.

Another reason for Russell's abandonment of the sensibilia theory was the sheer complexity and, as he came to see it, implausibility of the views he tried to formulate about private and public spaces, the relations between them, and the way sensibilia are supposed to occupy them. He makes passing mention of this cluster of problems in MPD, before there reporting, as his main reason for abandoning the attempt to construct 'matter out of experienced data alone', that it 'is an impossible programme . . . physical objects cannot be interpreted as structures composed of elements actually experienced' (MPD p. 79). This last remark is not strictly consistent with Russell's stated view in the original texts that sensibilia are not, and do not have to be, actually sensed; MPD gives a much more phenomenalistic gloss to the theory than it originally possessed. But it touches upon a serious problem with the theory: which is that it is at least problematic to speak of an 'unsensed sense-datum' which does not even require – as its very name seems *per contra* to demand – an intrinsic connection to perception.

In these early endeavours Russell gave only passing attention to other important questions in epistemology which he later, by contrast, came to emphasize. They concern the kind of reasoning traditionally supposed to be the mainstay of science, namely non-demonstrative inference. It was some years before Russell returned to consider these questions: the main discussion he gives is to be found in HK, but promissory notes are issued in AMt and IMT.

Acceptance of James's 'neutral monism' was an important turning point. Summarily stated, James's theory is that the world ultimately consists neither of mental stuff, as idealists hold, nor material stuff, as materialists hold, nor of both in problematic relation, as dualists hold, but of a neutral stuff from which the appearance of both mind and matter is formed. By Russell's own account, he was converted to this theory soon after finishing LLA. He had written about James's views in 1914, and rejected them; in LLA itself he was more sympathetic, though still undecided; but finally in a paper entitled 'On Propositions' (1919) he embraced the theory, and used it as a basis for AMi.

The question that came to seem key to Russell is whether consciousness is the essence of the mental, given that, in line with traditional views, consciousness is itself taken to be essentially intentional. In light of Russell's difficulties with the multiple relation theory of judgement it is pointful to remember its partial ancestry in Meinong's view that the intentional relation has at least the three elements of act, content and object. In accepting neutral monism Russell was abandoning the irreducible assumptions of any such view. First, he says, there is no such thing as the 'act'. The occurrence of the content of a thought is the occurrence of the thought, and there is neither empirical evidence nor theoretical need for an 'act' in addition. Russell's diagnosis of why anyone might think otherwise is that we say, '*I* think so-and-so', which suggests that thinking is an act performed by a subject. But he rejects this, for reasons similar to those advanced by Hume, who held that the notion of the self is a fiction, and that we are empirically licensed to say no more, on occasions of specifying them, than that there are bundles of thoughts.

Second, Russell criticizes the relation of content and object. Meinong and others had taken it that the relation is one of direct reference, but in Russell's view it is more complicated and derivative, consisting largely of beliefs about a variety of more and less indirect connections among contents, between contents and objects, and among objects. Add to this the fact that, in imagination and non-standard experiences like hallucination, one can have thoughts without objects, and one sees that the content–object relation involves many difficulties – not least, Russell says, in giving rise to the dispute between idealists who think that content is more significant than objects, and realists who think that objects are more significant than content. (Russell's use of these labels, although standard, is misleading: we should for accuracy substitute the label 'anti-realist' for 'idealist' here; this is because whereas, at bottom, realism and anti-realism are indeed differing theses about the relation of contents to objects, and thus are *epistemological* theses, idealism is a *metaphysical* thesis about the nature of the world; namely, that it is ultimately mental in character. This point is frequently missed in philosophical debate, so Russell is in good company.[10]) All these difficulties can be avoided, Russell claims, if we adopt a version of neutral monism.

James argued that the single kind of metaphysically ultimate raw material is arranged in different patterns by its interrelations, some of which we call 'mental' and some 'physical'. He attributed his view to dissatisfaction with theories of consciousness, which in his view are merely the wispy inheritors of old-fashioned talk about 'souls'. He agreed that thoughts exist; what he denied is that they are entities. They are, instead, functions: there is 'no aboriginal

---

10 See A. C. Grayling, 'Understanding Realism', in M. Marsonet (ed.), *Metaphysics and Logic*, Kluwer, forthcoming.

stuff or quality of being, contrasted with that of which mate-rial objects are made, out of which our thoughts of them are made; but there is a function in experience which thoughts perform, and for the performance of which this quality of being is invoked. That function is *knowing*.'[11]

In James's view the single kind of 'primal stuff', as he called it, is 'pure experience'. Knowing is a relation into which different portions of primal stuff can enter; the rela-tion itself is as much part of pure experience as its relata.

Russell could not go along with quite all of this. He thought that James's use of the phrase 'pure experience' showed a lingering influence of idealism, and rejected it; he preferred the use made by others of the term 'neutral-stuff', a nomenclatural move of importance because whatever the primal stuff is, it has to be able – when differently arranged – to give rise to what could not appropriately be called 'experi-ence', for example stars and stones. But even with this modified view Russell only partially agreed. He thought that it is right to reject the idea of consciousness as an entity, and that it is partly but not wholly right to consider both mind and matter as composed of neutral-stuff which in isolation is neither; especially in regard to sensations – an important point for Russell, with his overriding objective of marrying sense to physics. But he insisted that certain things belong

11 W. James, *Essays in Radical Empiricism*, New York: Longman Green & Co., 1912, pp. 3–4.

only to the mental world (images and feelings) and others only to the physical world (everything which cannot be described as experience). What distinguishes them is the kind of causality that governs them; there are two different kinds of causal law, one applicable only to psychological phenomena, the other only to physical phenomena. Hume's law of association exemplifies the first kind, the law of gravity the second. Sensation obeys both kinds, and is therefore truly neutral.

Adopting this version of neutral monism obliged Russell to abandon some of his earlier views. One important change was abandonment of 'sense-data'. He did this because sense-data are objects of mental acts, which he now rejected; therefore, since there can be no question of a relation between non-existent acts and supposed objects of those acts, there can be no such objects either. And because there is no distinction between sensation and sense-data – that is, because we now understand that the sensation we have in seeing, for example, a colour patch *just is* the colour patch itself – we need only one term here, for which Russell adopts the name 'percept'.

Before accepting neutral monism, Russell had objected to it on a number of grounds, one being that it could not properly account for belief. And as noted, even when he adopted the theory it was in a qualified form; mind and matter overlap on common ground, but each has irreducible aspects. Nevertheless what at last persuaded him was the fact, as it seemed to him, that psychology and physics had come very close: the new physics both of the atom and of relativistic space–time had effectively dematerialized matter, and psychology, especially in the form of behaviourism, had effectively materialized mind. From the internal viewpoint of introspection, mental reality is composed of sensations and images. From the external viewpoint of observation, material things are composed of sensations and sensibilia. A more or less unified theory therefore seems possible by treating the fundamental difference as one of arrangement: a mind is a construction of materials organized in one way, a brain more or less the same materials organized in another.

A striking feature of this view is, surprisingly, how idealist it is. Russell had, as noted, charged James with residual idealism. But here he is arguing something hardly distinguishable: that minds are composed of sensed percepts – *viz.* sensations and images – and matter is a logical fiction constructed of unsensed percepts. Now Russell had often insisted (using his earlier terminology) that sensibilia are 'physical' entities, in somewhat the sense in which, if one were talking about an item of sensory information in a nervous system, that datum would be present as impulses in a nerve or activity in a brain. But then nerves and brains, as objects of physical theory, are themselves to be understood as a constructions from sensibilia, not as traditionally understood 'material substance', the concept of which physics has shown to be untenable. At the end of AMi (pp. 305, 308) Russell accordingly says that 'an ultimate scientific account of what goes on in the world, if it were ascertainable, would resemble psychology rather than physics . . . [because] psychology is nearer to what exists'. This explains Russell's notorious claim that 'brains consist of thoughts' and that when a physiologist looks at another person's brain, what he 'sees' is a portion of his own brain.[12]

For robuster versions of materialism this aspect of Russell's view is hard to accept. But it is not the only difficulty with his version of neutral monism. Not least among others is the fact that he failed in his main aim, which was to refute the view that consciousness is essential to the distinction between mental and physical phenomena. He had not of course attempted to analyse consciousness quite away; his aim was rather to reduce its importance to the mind–matter question. But images, feelings and sensations, which play so central a role in his theory, stubbornly remain *conscious* phenomena, whereas the sensibilia (by definition including unsensed sensa) which constitute the greater part of matter are not. Russell accepted this, but tried to specify a criterion of difference which did not trade on these facts: namely, the criterion of membership of different causal realms. But whereas that difference is open to question – and even if it exists might be too often hard to see – the consciousness difference is clear cut. Relatedly, the intentionality which characterizes consciousness cannot be left out of accounts of

---

12 Schlipp, P., *The Philosophy of Bertrand Russell*, New York, 1963, p. 705.

knowledge; memory and perception are inexplicable without it. Russell later acknowledged this point, and gave it as a reason in MPD for having to return to the question of perception and knowledge in later writings.

He also later came to abandon the idea – anyway deeply unsatisfactory from the point of view of a theory supposed to be both *neutral* and *monist* – that images and feelings are essentially mental; that is, not wholly reducible to neutral-stuff, for in a very late essay he says, 'An event is not rendered either mental or material by any intrinsic quality, but only by its causal relations. It is perfectly possible for an event to have both the causal relations characteristic of physics and those characteristic of psychology. In that case, the event is both mental and material at once.'[13] This, for consistency, is what he should have argued in AMi itself, where only sensations have this character.

But this view in turn generates another problem, which is that it comes into unstable tension with a view to which Russell returned after AMi; namely, that the causes of percepts are inferred from the occurrence of the percepts themselves. As noted earlier, Russell wavered between treating physical things as logical constructions of sensibilia and as entities inferred as the causes of perception; he held this latter view in PP and returned to it after AMi. But on the face of it, one

---

13 'Mind and Matter', in *Portraits from Memory*, Simon and Schuster, 1958, p. 152.

is going to need a delicate connection between one's metaphysics and one's epistemology in order to hold both that minds and things are of one stuff, and that things are the unknown external inferred causes of what happens in minds. So those parts of the legacy of AMi which remain in his later thinking raise considerable difficulties for his views there about matter.

One of the chief reasons for Russell's reversion to a realistic, inferential view about physical things was the difficulty inherent in the notion of unsensed sensa or, in the later terminology, percepts. As noted above, the idea had been to replace inferred entities with logically constructed ones. If physical things can be logically constructed out of sensibilia, then two desiderata have been realized simultaneously: the theory is empirically based, and inferred entities have been shaved away by Ockham's Razor. But it is obvious that the idea of unsensed sensa (or unperceived percepts) is, if not indeed contradictory, at least problematic. It makes sense – although, without a careful gloss, it is metaphysically questionable – to talk of the existence of *possibilities* of sensation; but to talk of the existence of *possible sensations* arguably does not (recall Russell's definition of sensibilia as entities having the 'same metaphysical and physical status as sense-data without necessarily being data to any mind'.) If the choice lay between inferred material particulars and non-actual perceptions existing unperceived, it would seem best to accept the former. This is just what Russell himself came to think. But he did not return to the cruder form of inferential realism held in PP; he had something more ingenious – though in the end no more successful – up his sleeve.

Another reason for Russell's reversion to realism was his recognition that the notion of causality is problematic for phenomenalism. Things in the world seem to affect one another causally in ways hard to explain on the mere basis of reports of sense-experience. Moreover, a causal theory of perception is a natural and powerful way of explaining how experience itself arises. In Russell's mature philosophy of science, contained in AMt and HK, he did not opt for a Lockean view which says that our percepts resemble their causal origins, on the ground that we cannot be directly acquainted with things, and therefore cannot expect to know their qualities and relations. Rather, he now argued, changes in the world and our perceptions are correlated, or co-vary, at least for orders of things in the world that our perceptual apparatus is competent to register (we do not, for example, perceive electrons swarming in the table, so there is no associated covariation of world and perception at that level). The correspondence between percepts and things is one of *structure* at the appropriate level: 'Whatever we infer from perceptions it is only structure that we can validly infer; and structure is what can be expressed by mathematical logic' (AMt p. 254). And this means that we have to be 'agnostic' about all but the physical world's mathematical properties, which is what physics describes (AMt p. 270).

Russell had come to think that the best candidate for what is metaphysically most basic in the world is the 'event'. Objects are constructed out of events in the following way: the world is a collection of events, most of which cluster together around a multitude of 'centres', thus constituting individual 'objects'. Each cluster radiates 'chains' of events, which interact with and react upon chains radiating from other centres – among which are perceivers. When a chain interacts with the events constituting the perceptual apparatus of a perceiver, the last link in the chain is a percept. Since everything is ultimately constituted of events, they are in effect the 'neutral-stuff' of which minds and material things are made. Minds are clusters of events connected by 'mental' relations, not least among them memory; otherwise there is no metaphysical difference between mind and matter. Finally, the interrelations of event-chains is what scientific causal laws describe.

This view enabled Russell to formulate the argument he had long been trying to state satisfactorily: namely, that percepts are parts of things. For on this view it is not the case that there are events which constitute things, and then in addition other events which are perceptions of those things; rather, there are just events constituting the object, some of which are percepts – these being the terminal events of the chains radiating from the object which interact with events constituting the perceiver.

This theory is inferential not in the earlier sense in which the causes of percepts, lying inaccessibly beyond a veil of perception, are guessed from the nature of the percepts themselves. Rather, the inference is from certain terminal events, *viz.* percepts – which are interactions between (using the term heuristically) 'mental' events and that level of structure in the rest of the event-world with which the 'mental' events are capable of interacting – to the clusters and chains of events constituting the world as a whole.

In AMt the core of the theory is the idea that knowledge of the world is purely structural. We know the qualities and relations as well as the structure of percepts, but we know only the structure of external events, not their qualities. This seems somewhat reminiscent of Locke's distinction between primary and secondary qualities, but it is not; Russell is saying that all we can infer from our percepts is the structure of the qualities and relations of things, not the qualities and relations themselves; and that this is the limit of knowledge.

This theory has a fatal flaw, which was quickly recognized by the mathematician M. H. A. Newman and set out in an article published soon after the appearance of AMt. It is that since our knowledge of the structure of events is not a mere result of our stipulating them, but is manifestly non-trivial, it follows that our inferential knowledge cannot be limited solely to questions of structure. This is because – to put the point by a rough analogy – a number of different worlds could be abstractly definable as having the same structure, and if they were, knowledge of their structure alone could not separate them and in particular could not individuate the 'real' one. If science genuinely consists of discoveries about the world through observation and experiment, the distinction between what we observe and what we infer cannot therefore be collapsed into a distinction between pure structure and qualities.

Russell accepted Newman's point: 'You make it entirely obvious that my statements to the effect that nothing is known about the physical world except its structure are either false or trivial, and I am somewhat ashamed not to have noticed it myself.'

As repeatedly noted, the common thread linking Russell's earlier and later views is the aim of securing the move from perception to the objects of physical theory. On his view, this move must either be inferential, in which it takes us from the incorrigible data of sense to something else; or it is analytic, that is, consists in a process of constructing physical entities out of percepts. On the later view just reported, the inference has a special advantage over more usual inferential theories, in that the inference is not from one kind of thing to another, but from one part of something to its other parts.

In his earlier views Russell had accorded primary reality to sense-data and built everything else out of them. On the later view, reality belongs to events as the ultimate entities, and an important change of emphasis was introduced: percepts remain immediate and as certain as anything can be, but they are not construed as having accurately to represent the physical world, which, in the picture offered by science as the most powerful way to understand it, is anyway very different from how it appears.

Crucially, however, there remains a familiar and major problem about whether inferences from perception to the world are secure. A large part of Russell's aim in HK was to state grounds for taking them to be so. Throughout his thinking about the relation of perception and science he was convinced, as his above-quoted remark in the October 1912 letter to Ottoline Morrell shows, that something has to be known independently of experience for scientific knowledge to be possible. Earlier, as noted, he thought that purely logical principles provide such knowledge. But he now saw that logic alone is insufficient; we must know something more substantial. His solution was to say that inference from perception to events is justified in the light of certain 'postulates' which nevertheless state contingent facts about the word. So stated, Russell's view immediately reminds one of Kant's thesis that possession of 'synthetic *a priori* knowledge' is a condition of the possibility of knowledge in general, a view which Russell robustly dismissed in the Preface to HK. The difference is explained by the tentative and probabilistic account that Russell, in this last major attempt to state a theory of knowledge, felt was all that could be hoped for.

Two features of Russell's approach in HK explain this result. One is that he now thought that knowledge should be understood in 'naturalistic' terms; that is, as a feature of our biological circumstances, taken together with the way the world is constituted. The other is that he had come to make a positive virtue of the fact (which he always otherwise accepted) that contingent knowledge is never certain, but at best merely credible to some degree. This second point enters into the detailed working out of the views in HK. The first makes its appearance whenever Russell needs to justify the justifications which HK attempts to provide for scientific knowledge.

When data have a certain credibility independently of their relations to other data, Russell describes them as having a degree of 'intrinsic' credibility. Propositions having some intrinsic credibility lend support to propositions inferred from them. The chief question then becomes: how do propositions with some measure of intrinsic credibility transfer that credibility to the hypotheses of science? Another way of framing the question is to ask how reports of observation and experiment can function as evidence. This is where Russell's postulates come in.

There are five postulates. The first, 'the postulate of quasi-permanence', is intended to replace the ordinary idea of a persisting thing: 'Given any event A, it happens very frequently that, at any neighbouring time, there is at some neighbouring place an event very similar to A.' Thus the 'things' of common sense are analysed into sequences of similar events. The ancestor of this idea is Hume's analysis of the 'identity' of things in terms of our propensity to take a sequence of resembling perceptions to be evidence for a single thing, as when you have perceptions of a rose bush every time you go into the garden, and therefore take it that there is a single persisting rose bush there even when no perceivers are present.

The second, 'the postulate of separable causal lines', states that 'it is frequently possible to form a series of events such that, from one or two members of the series, something can be inferred as to all the other members'. For example, we can keep track of a billiard ball throughout a game of billiards; common sense thinks of the ball as a single thing changing its position, which according to this postulate is to be explained by treating the ball and its movements as a series of events from some of which you can infer information about the others.

The third is 'the postulate of spatio–temporal continuity', designed to deny 'action at a distance' by requiring that if there is a causal connection between two events that are not contiguous, there must be a chain of intermediate links between them. Many of our inferences to unobserved occurrences depend upon this postulate.

The fourth is 'the structural postulate', which states that 'when a number of structurally similar complexes are ranged about a centre in regions not widely separated, it is usually the case that all belong to causal lines having their origin in an event of the same structure at the centre'. This is intended to make sense of the idea that there exists a world of physical objects common to all perceivers. If six million people all listen to the Prime Minister's broadcast on the radio, and upon comparing notes find that they heard remarkably similar things, they are entitled to the view that the reason is the commonsense one that they all heard the same man speaking over the airwaves.

The fifth and last is 'the postulate of analogy', which states that 'given two classes of events A and B, and given that, whenever both A and B can be observed, there is reason to believe that A causes B, then if, in a given case, A is observed, but there is no way of observing whether B occurs or not, it is probable that B occurs; and similarly if B is observed, but the presence or absence of A cannot be observed'. This postulate speaks for itself (HK pp. 506–12).

The point of the postulates is, Russell says, to justify the first steps towards science. They state what we have to know, in addition to observed facts, if scientific inferences are to be valid. It is not advanced science which is thus justified, but its more elementary parts, themselves based on common-sense experience.

But what is the sense of 'know' here? On Russell's view, the knowing involved in 'knowledge of the postulates' is a kind of 'animal knowing', which arises as habitual beliefs from the experience of interaction with the world and experience in general. It is far from being certain knowledge. 'Owing to the world being such as it is,' Russell says, certain occurrences are sometimes, in fact, evidence for certain others; and owing to animals being adapted to their environment, occurrences which are, in fact, evidence of others tend to arouse expectation of those others. By reflecting on this process and refining it, we arrive at the canons of inductive inference. These canons are valid if the world has certain characteristics which we all believe it to have. (HK pp. 514–15)

These are the commonsense facts that the postulates in effect embody, and it is in this sense that we 'know' them. They are implied in the inferences we make, and our inferences are by and large successful; so the postulates can be regarded as in a sense self-confirming.

Although Russell thinks of the postulates as something we know *a priori*, it is clear that their status is odd. They are in fact empirical in one sense, since they either record or are suggested by experience. What gives them their *a priori* status is that they are *treated as known* independently of empirical confirmation (except indirectly in practice), rather than as generalizations in need of such justification. In effect Russell selected some general contingent beliefs which are especially useful to have as premises in thinking about the world, and elevated them to the dignity of postulates. Their indirect justification, in turn, is that on the whole they, or the results of their application, work. Allied to the extremely modest ambition Russell has for epistemology in HK this might be enough. But it has no pretensions to be a theory of know-ledge as traditionally conceived, nor a rigorous account of non-demonstrative reasoning.

These last remarks suggest why Russell's arguments in HK received little response, much to his disappointment. He rec-ognized well enough that canons of evidence and scientific reasoning are worth investigating only if we can be confident that, if we got them right, they would reliably deliver sci-ence. But the most that Russell's argument establishes is that, so far, the general principles on which our empirical thinking relies have been largely successful. But this looks like exactly the kind of unbuttressed inductive inference Russell was anxious to caution against, citing the example of the chicken who, on being fed day after day, grew increasingly pleased with the world – until the day the butcher came.

In particular, we have no guarantee against the possibility that use of the postulates leads to falsehood, either occasion-ally or in some systematic way. Now this possibility is in effect allowed by Russell in asking very little of epistemology. The complaint must therefore be that the argument in HK is in fact an admission of failure, when taken in the light of the epistemological tradition. Descartes and his successors in modern philosophy raised questions about the nature of knowledge and how we get it precisely so that they could distinguish between some enterprises – alchemy, astrology and magic, say – and others – chemistry, astronomy, and medicine, say – which differ not merely in the number of genuinely practical applications they offer, but in telling us something true about the world; and where, moreover, the latter fact explains the former, and opens the way to more of both by the same route. Moreover, our ancient prejudices and animal beliefs might be controverted in the process, as indeed happens: for the world depicted by science is remarkably different from the world of common sense. But Russell in HK says the utility of applications and those same animal habits of belief are the only final justification we can hope for in epistemology. This is very much less than the project of epistemology traditionally aims to achieve, and it is much less than Russell himself hoped to achieve on first launching his epistemological project after PM.

Russell had charged Kant with a 'Ptolemaic counter-revolution' in the Preface to HK, but it is not clear that HK itself escapes a Ptolemaic tinge. The postulates are expressly not transcendentally necessary framework features in any sense comparable to Kant's categorial concepts, or to any other species of foundational principle. They are in effect rules of thumb, 'distilled' as Russell puts it, from the epistemological pragmatics of common sense, and justified – if that is the right thing to expect them to be – by their manifest utility in scientific enquiry and ordinary life.

Nevertheless, they prompt two thoughts. One is that a solid argument can be given in favour of strengthening postulates of the kind envisaged by Russell into structural conditions of enquiry. For what are in effect temperamental reasons it was not open to Russell to consider investigating, by means of transcendental arguments, what is required for the possibility of the kind of knowledge in which science consists. No doubt the precipitate of something like the postulates would result; and that is a suggestive thought. Such an argument would be in fact Russellian, because it would follow his example in his earlier epistemological work of seeking the logical distribution of the problem, so to speak, as when, in the 1911–14 work, he distinguished what was logically primitive from what was derived from it, and how both parts of this classification related to one another in the structure they formed.

It is of course no more than a coincidence, but a remarkable one, that at the time Russell was writing HK, Wittgenstein was coming to not dissimilar conclusions in *On Certainty* – as if they had been travelling different routes and arriving at near-points at the end of the journey. Wittgenstein's late interest in problems of scepticism and knowledge is rather striking in being straightforward workaday philosophy of just the kind he earlier dismissed as fly-in-the-bottle. His interest in epistemology therefore looks like acceptance that philosophical problems are real ones after all, amenable to investigation – and even *solution*.[14] His contribution is to insist on the internal connection between the concepts of

14 See A. C. Grayling, 'Wittgenstein on Knowledge and Certainty', in H. Glock, *Wittgenstein: A Critical Reader*, Routledge, 2001.

knowing and doubting, and equally to insist that epistemic justification is provided by the conceptual scheme within which talk of knowledge and doubt alone gets content. The similarities between the very late Russell and Wittgenstein lie in the thought that (to put the matter neutrally as between them) a given area of discourse requires that we accept certain things in order to be able to get along in it – the 'grammatical' propositions which key a discourse's sense, in Wittgenstein; the postulates required by inquiry, for Russell. Of course the parallel is not direct, but it is suggestive.

CHAPTER 3

Russell's Transcendental Argument in *An Essay on the Foundations of Geometry*[1]

Russell was generous in attributing the sources of his inspiration to others, and never more so than in explaining what he described as the 'revolution' in his philosophical thought which occurred in the closing years of the nineteenth century. At Cambridge he had been made to feel the influence of Kant and Hegel, and especially of the latter, with whom he sided whenever he encountered disagreement between them. His great plan for two series of books effecting a synthesis of philosophy and science was Hegelian in inspiration, and his Fellowship dissertation, *An Essay on the Foundations of Geometry*, was Kantian not just in inspiration but in aim and, to a significant degree, content also.

---

1   The immediate ancestor of this paper was read under the title 'Russell, Moore and the Flight from Kant' at the Russell Conference, University of Southampton, 1995. I am grateful to those who attended for comments.

Russell gave the credit for the revolution in his thought to Moore: 'Moore led the way but I followed in his footsteps.[2] Several times he cites Moore's paper 'The Nature of Judgment' as the key document in this change.[3] Commenting on its influence, he says that its most important doctrine is its realist commitment to the independence of fact from experience. But each of them pursued differently emphasized routes from this agreement: Moore was concerned to refute idealism, while Russell was more interested in refuting monism. Nevertheless Russell took these two -isms to be connected through the doctrine of relations. In his view monism arises from commitment to the view that all relations are grounded in their terms; the application to idealism is that relations between thought or experience and their objects are asserted to be internal likewise, rendering them interdependent in ways that make what we pretheoretically take to be *objective* relata in some sense mental or grounded in the mental.

So much is familiar enough. But there is reason to think that another paper Moore published in 1899 had as big an effect on Russell from the viewpoint of what one might call its reach into Russell's later philosophical work. This is Moore's Critical Notice of Russell's *Essay on the Foundations of Geometry* (here-

---

2   *My Philosophical Development* (hereafter MPD), p. 42.
3   Critical notice of Russell's *An Essay on the Foundations of Geometry, Mind*, 1899.

after EFG). One is tempted to compare it in character and effect to Frege's celebrated conversion of Husserl from psychologism by his review of Husserl's *Philosophie der Arithmetik*. This would not be gathered from MPD, where Russell dismisses the argument of EFG on the grounds that the General Theory of Relativity made it obsolete. But when one considers what Russell says in *Human Knowledge, Its Scope and Limits* about Kant and about the postulates of scientific inference, one sees that the revolution in his philosophical views as profoundly rooted out the temptations of transcendental philosophy as it did monism – but, it might be argued, hardly with so positive an effect, because Russell ended by believing that there can be no *ultimate* appeal to *a priori* knowledge in the constitution of knowledge in general: hence the tottering version of fallibilism in *Human Knowledge,* with its ultimate reliance on supposed contingencies about evolution and animal habits. The flight from sophisticated psychologism had, so to say, crash-landed in crude biologism. Note, however, that Russell says in a letter to Moore of 18 July 1899: 'I had not written to you about your review, because on all important points I agreed with it.' Thereafter he made no more use of Kantian strategies and took to calling him by Cantor's disagreeable label for him, 'Yon sophistical Philistine'.

Yet in EFG Russell not only employs a transcendental argument of great interest, but gives a characterization of the nature of transcendental arguments which is of even greater interest. On the first head: it is noteworthy that espousing or rejecting some version of the transcendentalist strategy in *something* like Kant's sense (one need not accept much else of the Kantian luggage; compare Strawson's selectivity in *The Bounds of Sense*) is a matter quite independent of espousal or rejection of either or both of pluralism and realism, the two commitments which mark Russell's philosophy after EFG. If Russell had not lumped everything Kantian together for wholesale rejection, but had made use of transcendental arguments as he subtly understood them in EFG, he might have spared himself the later epistemological insecurities he variously suffered. On the second head: as is characteristic of Russell, his account of the nature of transcendental arguments in EFG anticipates later revived interest in the strategy, not only as Strawson and some others of us have deployed them, but in variant forms; as, for example, in the generalized notion of presuppositions, whose role in the solution of certain semantic problems was later to return to haunt Russell.

Russell's insight into the transcendental strategy is well brought out by Moore's interesting failure to understand it, which is why I enter his account via Moore's devastating-seeming attack in the Critical Notice of EFG.[4] In recent major studies of Russell both Nick Griffin and Peter Hylton[5] give it

---

4   Russell's *An Essay*.

5   N. Griffin, *Russell's Idealist Apprenticeship*, Clarendon Press, 1991; P. Hylton, *Russell, Idealism, and the Emergence of Analytic Philosophy*, Clarendon Press, 1990.

attention, the former as part of his detailed account of Russell on geometry and the latter more briefly as constituting an attack on psychologism, which in important part it was indeed intended to be; but Hylton leaves aside questions about the merits of Moore's attack, and whether Russell should have capitulated to it so entirely – bearing in mind that, as Russell saw and indeed insisted, the philosophical consequences of theories of geometry are not confined to choice of geometry for physical theory, but impinge significantly on our theories of perceptual experience, representation and indexical thought.[6] On this question Griffin takes the view that the jury remains out on whether Russell's way with the Kantian strategy – in particular, his reworking of a transcendental argument to the necessity for experience of a 'form of externality' – is in any degree successful.[7] I am inclined to think that it indeed has something to offer: but in proceeding by way of a discussion of the merits of Moore's attack on EFG I shall, except in relation to one matter, only obliquely indicate part of why that is so.

---

6   I.e., we need to know – granted that perceived space is not purely Euclidean – something about what is philosophically at stake for our thinking about perceptual space in theories of geometry in relation to (a) its role in indexical modes of thought, and (b) its relation to the space or space-time of our best current theories about the structure and properties of the physical world, etc.

7   Griffin, *Russell's Idealist Apprenticeship*, p. 132.

It is useful to have a reminder of what Russell was attempting in EFG. His aim was to survey the foundations of geometry in the light of the revolutionary advances in that science since Kant. Kant had claimed that space is the form of outer sensibility, and that Euclidean geometry describes it; but nineteenth-century mathematicians called into question both the belief that space is Euclidean and the claim that a Euclidean form of space is necessary to outer experience. Moreover they showed that Euclidean (space has zero curvature), Lobatchevskyan (with Gauss and Bolyai: hyperbolic geometry – space has negative curvature), Riemannian (spherical or double elliptic – space has positive curvature) and Kleinian (single elliptic) geometries can be derived as special cases of projective geometry, which deals with the qualitative (descriptive) properties of space, whereas Euclidean and the other non-Euclidean basic geometries deal with its quantitative (metric) properties. So a set of properties not recognized in Euclidean geometry – namely, the qualitative ones – had been shown to be logically prior to Euclidean properties. The question of what, if anything, constitutes the *a priori* foundation of geometrical knowledge therefore needed to be considered afresh, and this task Russell undertook in EFG.

Russell accepted the Kantian view that there must be such a thing as a 'form of externality' as a condition of possibility for spatial experience. In an interesting modification of Kant's thesis he argued that the possibility of such experience rests not just on the constitution of sensibility but on the world's receptiveness to the adjectives we impose on it. But he locates the properties of the form of externality not in Euclidean but in projective geometry, its transcendental status – carefully disentangled from the question of the *subjectivity* of *a priori* elements in experience – consisting in its applying to all spaces independently of experience of any of them.

The chief argument is that qualitative relations must be prior to quantitative ones. There are four fundamental qualitative principles:

1. all parts of space are homogeneous; that is, are qualitatively similar, and all are relative, that is, lie outside one another;
2. space is continuous and infinitely divisible, with the point as the limit of infinite divisibility;
3. two points determine a straight line, three points not on a line determine a plane, and so on for higher figures; and
4. the dimension of space must be finite.

Certain refinements of these constitute further *a priori* principles required for metrical geometry – required because measurement presupposes them. Homogeneity of space becomes free mobility (analytically equivalent to the constant curvature of space); and the 'two points–straight line' principle becomes an axiom about distance. (These principles are presupposed by measurement, and turn out to lie in the domain of metageometry, and therefore to apply to physical space.) Russell concluded that because these geometries are the only mathematically possible ones whose spaces are homogeneous, they are the only ones that can apply to physical space. Therefore physical space must be one of Euclidean, Lobatchevskyan, Riemannian or Kleinian. On empirical grounds Russell said that it is Euclidean.

Two developments subsequent to the writing of EFG rendered its views, as Russell says, obsolete. One, the development of topology – which generalizes on projective as projective had generalized on Euclidean geometry – imposes an obligation on any Kantians staying the course to review afresh the question of what, if any, geometrical principles are *a priori*. But much more seriously, every feature of the four-dimensional, non-Euclidean, non-homogeneous (not having a constant curvature) space of the General Theory of Relativity had been effectively or explicitly denied by Russell, who had not registered Riemann's point that a belief in the constant curvature of space depends upon ignoring the existence of matter. When matter is taken into account, homogeneity disappears, as the General Theory states (matter is absorbed into the geometry of space–time which therefore varies regionally according to the matter in it).[8]

---

8   There is a useful survey in Morris Kline's 'Introduction' to the edition of EFG published by Dover in 1956.

The fourth and final chapter of EFG contains the discussion of the philosophical aspects of these views which interest us here, because it is these that Moore attacks. Here Russell argues that the *a priori* axioms of geometry can be deduced from the form of externality as a transcendental ground of experience – that is, the condition of the possibility of experience (see esp. section 189, EFG). Russell's view differs in significant ways from Kant's, especially in the interesting respect that it requires the mutual externality of things presented in sense-perception rather than (to begin with anyway) the externality of things to the Self. This and other points in Russell's account are independently interesting and perhaps important for theories of perceptual representation, which makes them worth pursuing on their own account.

Russell defined the *a priori* as that which is logically presupposed in experience, where (as Hylton reminds us)[9] the force of 'logically' is the Kantian transcendental one in which questions about the conditions of the possibility of experience are at stake. But whereas for Kant these were *synthetic* judgements only – for him, analytic ones follow from the principle of contradiction alone – for Russell this division will not do, and along with other post-Kantians he rejected it.[10] But he also objected to the conflation of the *a priori* with subjectivity, on the grounds that it places *a priori*

---

9 Hylton, *Russell*, pp. 73–6.
10 Hylton, *Russell*, pp. 75–6.

truth at the mercy of empirical psychology,[11] and so a second import of Russell's use of 'logically' is its marking a refusal to accept that the validity of Euclid waits upon empirical facts about human spatial intuition.[12]

Russell's argument goes as follows. Knowledge starts from sense experience, the objects of sense experience are complex, whatever is complex has parts, parts have to be mutually external to one another, and therefore a form of externality is logically prior to experience. This form of externality cannot be purely temporal, for the reason – among others – that things given in experience must be 'various' or 'diverse' to allow for complexity, and one crucial way in which they are so is by occupying different positions in space – hence space as the form of externality required. The notion of a form of externality is an essentially relative one; nothing can be external to itself, and so for any one thing there must be another thing to which it is external; the externality is of course mutual, and there have to be yet other positions from which the positions they occupy in turn differ. (The second main contention of EFG is that geometry contains contradictions: this is the Hegelian aspect of the thesis. I leave this aside; see Hylton).[13]

Moore took himself to have two fatal objections to Rus-

---

11 EFG3; Hylton, *Russell*, p. 76.
12 EFG93; Hylton, *Russell*, p. 77.
13 Hylton, *Russell*, pp. 84 *et seq.*

sell's project. One is that the most that could be established by an argument of this kind is something about what is presupposed to the kind of experience we in fact have, and that therefore the argument is philosophically valueless because it tells us only about certain psychological contingencies.

The other is less easy to state briefly. Russell said that an *a priori* judgement is one whose truth-value is insensitive to empirical considerations, and can only be rendered false 'by a change which should render some branch of experience formally impossible, i.e. inaccessible to our methods of cognition' (EFG p. 60). Moore seems to have taken Russell to be saying that there is something – a subject matter of some sort – to which cognitive access can be had only if a certain *a priori* judgement is true; and that the judgement's being rendered false would be the effect of the necessary falsehood of judgements about that subject matter; to which Moore responded, 'That which is "inaccessible to our methods of cognition" would seem only to mean that which we cannot know; it cannot imply that the judgements in question cannot be true' (Moore 398). Moore labels the conflation of questions about what is true with what can be known as the 'Kantian fallacy'.[14] In his view it is for psychology to answer

---

14 Compare Frege on exactly the same point. Anti-psychologism was in the air after Kant's and post-Kantian attacks on psychologism: Kant himself criticized the empiricists' psychologism in basing truth on experience in the way they did.

questions about what and how we know, so such questions are philosophically irrelevant.[15] The crucial commitment in this view is to the independence of judgements from thought: hence the reason for Russell's citing Moore's other 1899 paper, 'The Nature of Judgment' (hereafter NJ),[16] as the engine in their break with the Kantian and Hegelian traditions (in 'The Nature of Judgment' Moore specifically addressed himself to Bradley's views).

There is much to contest here. The two points Moore addresses are intimately connected in Russell's strategy, in a way that Moore fails to see. He misunderstands the second of them – the one about the presuppositional relationship – and opposes to it a familiar realist claim, the argument for which, offered in NJ, is inadequate (there might be better arguments for it, but Moore does not give them). He does, however, see that the first part of Russell's argument requires a particular supplementation, the satisfaction of an ancillary requirement, one which involves a break with Kant on an important matter and which, on the face of it, seems impossibly difficult to give. Russell evidently took Moore's argument on this point to be conclusive in view of his complete abandonment of the Kantian enterprise.

I take the second point first, concerning the relation of *a priori* judgements to the branches of experience which pre-

---

15 Cf. Wittgenstein in the *Tractatus*.
16 Russell's *An Essay on the Foundations of Geometry*, *Mind*, 1899.

suppose them. Moore seems to be confused about what Russell is claiming here. He seems to take Russell's claim to be that unless such judgements are true, judgements about the subject matter in question must be false (taking the modalities seriously). Moore thus reads 'inaccessible to cognition' as implying that *there is* something about which we are not in a position to make judgements. His realist commitment to the independence of judgements from knowledge of their truth or falsity accordingly portrays this as a straightforward mistake. But Russell is not saying this; his claim is the familiar Kantian one that there could be no such branch of experience as the one in question unless we know *a priori* the judgements that make it possible. He put the point by saying that the only thing that could make such *a priori* judgements false is if the branch of experience in question were impossible; again taking the incorporated modalities seriously, his talk of the 'inaccessibility to cognition' of a branch of experience is not to be read as implying or (as Moore sees it) conceding that there is something to be known if only we could get at it; this is Moore's mistake. Rather, it says that if nothing constitutes the *a priori* condition of possibility for there being such cognition, there could be no such subject matter.

Russell's point here in fact concerns the very nature of transcendental arguments. He offers a novel and interesting way of capturing what is essential about such arguments, which, contrary to what is often thought, are not in the least logically peculiar or special, but are distinguished from other argumentative strategies by a certain distinctive aim, which is to establish conceptual title to a principle or claim which, accepted as true, licenses our activity in some region of judgement (and I intend that to be a terminological variant for 'makes a certain kind of experience possible'). Kant is somewhat to blame for leading some commentators – in this connection I have Griffin in mind, who in his discussion of Moore on Russell's EFG expects more from transcendental arguments without quite saying what – to think that transcendental arguments have to take us beyond their premises, which concern the nature of a certain kind of experience (or thought), and establish something not already implicit in its character and conditions. But the attempt to show that we have a title to some principle or claim proceeds exactly by showing that we could not do something we in fact do – enjoy spatial sense-perception for example – unless a condition for doing so were satisfied; from which it follows that the principle is satisfied. For Kant as for Russell in EFG the spotlight of attention is on the conditions, because once the deduction of title (the legal metaphor was consciously intended by Kant) has been achieved, the next step is to note that, since the judgement – whose acceptance as true is a condition for the experience in question – could not itself have been derived from that experience but is logically anterior to it, it is *a priori*: and part of their transcendental task was to identify what has to be known *a priori* as a ground for that experience.

Put in the most schematic way, transcendental arguments state that there would not be A unless there were B, and that since there is A, there is B. Familiarly and prosaically, the underlying move is a statement of necessary conditionality: B is a necessary condition for A, and since A is the case, so therefore is B. (If one said: therefore B has to be the case too, the 'has to' has to be understood purely conditionally.) Arguments of this form are very common; they only cause a stir when applied in what might be called Kantian contexts. Russell in EFG succeeded in capturing their character by casting them as portrayals of presuppositionality in terms of truth-value, partially (but only partially: see below) anticipating later variants of the move. We see this by noting Moore's mistake in taking Russell to have asserted that there is a presuppositional relation between A and B such that if judgements as to B are false, those as to A must be necessarily false. This makes the relation very peculiar, for it issues in the necessary falsehood of A-judgements when B-judgements are false – which it is not clear how one might motivate. But the mistake takes us close to what Russell intended. In later debate, presupposition is more familiarly (if no less problematically) taken as a relation obtaining between judgements such that a given presupposing judgement has a truth-value only if a given presupposed judgement is true (I am adhering here to the Russell–Moore terminology of the day: *mutatis mutandis*, the same points can be made in more careful ways, thus bringing out the fact that it is as a semantic relation that the notion is now standardly understood – rather than an epistemic one between, on the one hand, an asserter or judger seeking to assert or judge a content p and, on the other, another content q required for p's being assertable or judgeable as true or false). This is only part of what Russell intends, for the good reason that it is only part of what is implied in a transcendental argument, in which a stronger claim is at stake, namely, that the falsity of a given judgement – a B-judgement, say – renders impossible even the circumstances for making or entertaining a would-be A-judgement, a matter far antecedent to the would-be A-judgement's having a truth-value. So on the Kantian view, B's being true makes A either true or false; but B's being false makes it impossible to make or even entertain A-type judgements. Moore took it that Russell meant that B's being false makes A-judgements necessarily false. But the two claims are of course very different, and it is unclear whether what Moore imputes to Russell is even coherent. Russell, however, gives us an insight into the style of argument at stake.

In the foregoing there is no suggestion that either Moore or Russell had anticipated exactly what has come to be meant by talk of 'presupposition' since Pears and Strawson; rather, their debate illustrates the sense in which that later debate itself captures something close to but weaker than the relation which a transcendental argument asserts to hold between a given kind of experience (or conceptual practice) and what makes it possible. But in the uncertain oscillation between talk of experience and talk of judgements as we find it in Russell and Moore, it is easy to see that in one mode the appropriate locution is 'ground of possibility' and in the other, talk about the condition for possession by a judgement of truth-value as lying in the truth-value of another judgement. The two jargons are not the same in meaning, but once that is recognized there are no irreducible difficulties in straying between them as our protagonists do.

It is worth remarking at this juncture that this account of Moore's attack does not agree with the accounts given by Hylton and Griffin. On the reading we each give of Moore there might be a little latitude for interpretation because of the unclarities in Moore's presentation, but not that much: and Griffin, as noted, misidentifies the character of the transcendental strategy in general and Russell's in particular, chiefly by asking too much of it. I defer an itemized comparison here. But the crucial respect in which I hope that this supplements their discussions is in recognizing that the more significant argument of Moore's is the one directed not against the style of argument Russell uses, but against the argument itself: this occurs as the first point criticized by Moore above, together with its all-important ancillary requirement.

It is also worth noting at this juncture the argument Moore gives in NJ for the realist commitment he opposes to what he takes to be Russell's point here. It is remarkably implausible. Writing of 'the nature of a proposition or judgement' Moore says,

A proposition is composed not of words, nor yet of thoughts, but of concepts. Concepts are possible objects of thought; but that is no definition of them. It merely states that they may come into relation with a thinker; and in order that they *may* do anything, they must already *be* something. It is indifferent to their nature whether anybody thinks them or not. (NJ p. 179)

'Concepts form a *genus per se*, irreducible to anything else' (NJ pp. 178–9). This Platonism about concepts itself seems to be enthymematically premised, among other things, on the view that relations of acts of judging to their contents are external. But nothing is offered in support of that claim, and no other reason – of the better kinds needed – is offered for hypostasizing concepts and judgements. Since Moore goes on to assert that the world is made of concepts, thus realistically conceived, some such argument is surely called for. (In Frege, one at least has a strong motivation for assigning thoughts to a Platonistically conceived Third Realm, namely that the publicity constraints on sense require that it have a greater degree of objectivity than mappings across the psychological states of language users can yield. I argue elsewhere that Frege's requirement, backed as it is in this coherent way, is over strong.)[17]

---

17 'Publicity, Stability and Knowing the Meaning', in A. C. Grayling and P. Kotatko, *Meaning*, forthcoming.

Russell's transcendental argument has it, as we saw, that a form of externality is necessary for the possibility of experience, because the givens of experience are complexes; that is, have parts which must be external to each other. Moore's first point is directed at this proposition. He quotes Russell's claim that necessity always involves a ground, and says,

> But this ground must itself either be simply categorical, or else it must itself be necessary and require a further ground. In the former case we are actually trying to deduce an *a priori* proposition from one that, as categorical, is merely empirical; in the latter, which Mr Russell seems in the end inclined to accept, we must either allow an infinite regress of necessary propositions, and thus never reach the absolutely *a priori*, or else we must accept the view that knowledge is circular, and shall in the end return to the proposition from which we started as empirical, as being itself the ground of necessity of the *a priori*, and therefore itself as much *a priori* as the latter. Mr Russell seems actually to accept this latter view [pp. 57–60] – a view which renders his logical criterion nugatory, since it asserts that that which is presupposed in the empirical equally and in the same sense presupposes the empirical.

Moore is here arguing in effect that, leaving aside a regress of conditions which never terminates in an absolute *a priori*, however one otherwise tries to state the case the starting point is the nature of experience and the conclusion concerns what is required for it to be thus and so; and therefore 'to show that a "form of externality" is necessary for the possibility of experience, can only mean to show that it is presupposed in our actual experience' (CN p. 399). And Moore immediately sees that 'this can never prove that no experience would be possible without such a form, unless we assume that our actual experience is necessary, i.e. that no other experience is possible' (CN p. 399).

It no more occurred to Moore to consider whether this ancillary requirement can be met than, evidently, it occurred to Russell, who like most Kantians might have simply accepted that Kant was right to allow the possibility of other forms of experience – for example, he allowed that animals might have forms of spatial experience quite different from ours. For this reason Moore read Russell as having to find another way out for the argument, and therefore attributes to him what he calls the 'subterfuge' (CN p. 399) of the presuppositional argument. Moore thus views Russell's point about presuppositions as an *ad hoc* step taken to avoid a difficulty, not as a characterization of the argument to the necessity of a form of externality itself. As we saw, in this he is wrong. For it is of the essence of a transcendental argument that, in identifying what is necessarily presupposed to something which is the case, it tells us something else about what is the case as its condition. Instead of being a criticism of Russell's strategy, Moore's anatomization describes it.

But it does show that the condition identified as necessary for spatial experience is relative unless the ancillary requirement be met that no alternative experience is possible. At first sight this seems to pose too tall an order. But subsequent debate in philosophy has provided an interesting if controversial means of showing that there might indeed be a way to satisfy the requirement. (A polite form of execratory howl usually greets this assertion, chiefly because of now orthodox assumptions about possibility. When possibility is understood as an epistemic notion – as conceivability, in other words – the task is recognizably much more manageable. But the argument I'm about to borrow does not require a demonstration that most philosophers until the time of Kant were right to construe the modalities – all of them – as epistemic notions.) The argument, furnished by Davidson, is his celebrated case for saying that the idea of alternative conceptual schemes is incoherent. It has more texture than I am going to bring out here,[18] but in any case I only need its bones for present purposes. The argument goes as follows.

The idea of 'other ways of having experience' can be generalized into the idea of alternative conceptual schemes – alternative, that is, to our own, for arbitrarily constrained 'us'

18   I give it an extended discussion and proposed modification elsewhere; see my *Refutation of Scepticism*, Duckworth, 1985.

(it does not matter how restrictive one is about who 'we' are in talk of 'our' conceptual scheme, for the argument goes through whatever one says about this) – and conceptual schemes can be provided with criteria of identity by identifying them with languages or sets of intertranslatable languages. Then, in turn, questions about the possibility of the existence of conceptual schemes other than our own, perhaps existing undetectably from the point of view of our own, can be framed in terms of translatability. In this idiom, the question of whether there can be *other* or *alternative* schemes comes down to the question of whether there can be languages that we cannot translate. But since we can have no grounds for treating as a language anything that cannot be translated into our own language – since, in effect, the criterion of languagehood is 'translatability into a familiar idiom' – and since intertranslatability defines membership of the same scheme, the conception of distinct schemes – in particular, of mutually inaccessible schemes – is seen to be incoherent. But to say that there can be no such thing as an alternative scheme is, transposing back into the idiom of ways of experiencing, to say that ours can be – still taking our modalities seriously – the only such way. The argument is a strongly anti-relativist one; which is appropriate, because Moore's rebuttal of Russell's project takes precisely the form of a sceptical counter-claim to the effect that forms of experience are relative. As is usual, no argument is offered for the claim: its sole ground seems to be the now orthodox view of possibility mentioned.

One characteristic reaction to this application of the Davidson argument – here cavalierly seeming to keep the 'Ptolemaic counter-revolution' going – is to say that no contradiction infects the idea of something which is recognizably an untranslatable language. The usual example offered is the Minoan linear script. A response to this example is to point out that the inaccessibility here at issue is not to a language but to a script embodying a fragment of what we suppose to be a language, and moreover one not in use, which places a contingent barrier to translation which by itself is not relevant to the question of its languagehood. But another, more general, response is to contrast the notion of an untranslat*able* language with that of an untranslat*ed* language. Contingent barriers to translation of one established language into another (such as the current but, I surmise, reducible inability of most of us here to translate Magyar into English) do not, obviously, put them beyond the pale of languagehood; which tells us much, on reflection, about what would. Rather, the accessibility point rests on these general thoughts: that the concept of differences between languages, or schemes, or ways of having experience, essentially trades upon there being enough access between supposed alternatives for the differences to be apparent. There has to be a background of shared assumptions and beliefs giving rise to the degree of mutual comprehensibility which alone makes differences recognizable. And this is not a point about mere cultural relativities – about what might be called anthropological divergences, differences of opinion and high-level social practices – but about the most basic levels of cognitive activity turning on individuation, reference, property attribution and assent. In the fuller treatment of these points referred to above, I argue that this shared basis has to be rather rich and fine-grained, to the extent that it rules out indeterminacy of reference.[19] As applied to the question of language, one can connect points about shared background beliefs and holdings-true as a condition of getting translation started, with points about the recognizability of devices in the language for reference, predication and assent and dissent: so a much more articulated grasp of an alien tongue is required even by Quine's philosophical anthropologist before he can fairly get going. Alternatively put, the requirement for starting a translation manual is that there should already be one available.

Another response to these claims is that there are certain identifiable possessors of conceptual schemes which are not possessors of language, for example cats and cows, so the identification of schemes and languages fails, and with it the putative access required and therefore afforded by translation. One can leave aside the short answer from the inescapability of 'reading-in' in such cases – which might be (so say those who do not belong to a cat) what our attribution of

---

19   Cf Grayling, *Refutation of Scepticism*, chapter 3 *passim*.

concept-possession to languageless creatures consists in. We can leave this aside because it is obvious that one can give a strongly motivated and cogent argument for attributing concept-possession and attitudes, at least to a certain level of complexity (remembering the strictures of Frege and Wittgenstein on this subject), to at least the higher mammals, among other things on the grounds of the successful pragmatics attached to doing so: as witness Fodor's cat. The point might be put by saying that much of what can be attributed concerning the beliefs and intentions of such mammals is representable in one's own language in statements having as good a chance of being true on the evidence as those about creatures capable of making their own avowals. On this head, there is nothing second class about third-party attribution.

These points are made, remember, in response to questions about the intrinsic merits of Moore's attack on EFG, and whether Russell was without recourse in defending the philosophical strategy there adopted. These points at least show that both Moore and Russell were too swift here. And this can be substantiated by noting that there is of course a similar but much weaker response, or set of responses, that can be made to this aspect of Moore's criticism. As Strawson has argued (in *Scepticism and Naturalism* and elsewhere) there is much to be gained from an investigation of what our kind of experience requires, even if it is not the only kind there can be. This either allows philosophical interest to what

Moore dismisses as merely parochial, or it refuses to interpose so impermeable a membrane between psychological and philosophical considerations as was all the rage at the turn of the century. But in the presence of a stronger argument for the cogency of the general enterprise – I do not say, Kant's or Russell's in particular – it is worth contesting Moore's rejection of their style of argument more vigorously.

It might be asked what difference would have been made, outside his philosophy of mathematics, if Russell had retained some part of his early convictions about *a priori* knowledge. With the exception granted, one answer is: less than one might suppose, since it would not have interfered with his pluralism, his atomism or with his adoption of certain sustainable versions of non-Platonic realism; and another answer is that it might have offered resources to his epistemology from the lack of which they badly suffer. This is well illustrated by one salient consequence of dispensing with *a priori* constituents in knowledge, namely, Russell's reliance on the notion of acquaintance. His response to Moore's Platonism about concepts and judgements – which remained when the objects of acquaintance had become simultaneously far more various and refined – was to treat our relation to them as direct, theory-free, unmediated and conditionless. The relation is curiously thin and undefined; it comes without constraints, as if it were primitive; and insofar as it admits of being described as a mental operation, it is distinctively passive – the very opposite, one might say, of a relation in thought or experience in which some act – of perceiving or judging – plays a constitutive or partly constitutive role with respect to its objects. Now one need not be interested in specifically Kantian strategies for understanding how this works to feel the deficiency in the theory of acquaintance. One thing one can safely say is that if he had not abandoned the approach in EFG so entirely, Russell would have written differently later about knowledge and perception.

One of the really interesting features of EFG is that in it Russell is not an idealist; he as an anti-realist. (So is Kant in fact, on a certain best reading.) The differences are considerable. Idealism is a metaphysical thesis which asserts that reality is fundamentally mental; it is a Mind (e.g. Bradley) or it consists of minds and their ideas (e.g. Berkeley). Anti-realism is an epistemological thesis, which asserts that the relations between thought and its objects, perception and its accusatives, experience and its targets, language and the world, or whichever of these (different) pairings one takes as the focus, is not external, as realists claim. To say that the relations in question are internal is far from saying that thought or experience *creates* the world or is in some other way ontologically responsible for them: that is metaphysics, and specifically idealist metaphysics. Talk of the nature of the relations between mind and world is purely epistemological; it is not of course independent of considerations about what there is, but it does not by itself involve constitutive ontological claims. Now, Russell did not see the difference, so his unpreparedness to defend against Moore's attacks on *idealism* led him to abandon his *anti-realism*, a much more moderate position which he replaced, at first, with a very immoderate realism. It is the anti-realist features of Russell's thought in EFG which would have served his later epistemology well.

PART II

TWO VARIETIES OF NATURALISM

CHAPTER 4

Wittgenstein on Scepticism and Certainty

Wittgenstein's *On Certainty* (hereafter OC) is a collection of provisional notes, recording a journey, not an arrival.[1] But it is not difficult to see an intended destination for the journey, nor is there anything obscure about the territory being travelled. Yet OC has some surprising and unexpected features. For one thing, it recapitulates certain old attitudes in Wittgenstein, harking back to, but making different use of, Kantian traces in the *Tractatus*, here in the form of a roughly sketched (and possibly naturalistic) anti-realism similar in striking respects to Kant's empirical realism. For another thing, it appears to represent Wittgenstein's acceptance, at last, of philosophy's legitimacy as an enterprise. In all his earlier work he explicitly premised the claim that philosophy is a spurious enterprise, arising from misunderstandings

---

1   Selections from OC constitute chapter 13 of *The Wittgenstein Reader*, page references to which occur as WR in what follows. I refer frequently to paragraphs of OC not reprinted in WR.

about language. In OC he takes a central, traditional philosophical problem – the problem of scepticism and knowledge –
and tries to formulate a refutation of scepticism, and a characterization of knowledge and its justification. And he does this
by engaging with another attempt to do so, namely Moore's.

In order to evaluate the ideas it contains I shall therefore
take OC at face value – as an unfinished enquiry, the ideas in
which nevertheless strongly indicate the finished theses it
works towards – and proceed as follows.

First, there are two main themes in OC, which are, at the
least, not comfortably consistent with each other. One is a
reply to scepticism, and as such contributes recognizably to
the theory of knowledge. Indeed it is a reinvention almost
from scratch of views familiar, and usually more fully argued,
elsewhere in philosophy, of a broadly foundationalist stamp.
In this respect it carries forward, or unfolds, themes already
suggested in the *Philosophical Investigations* (henceforth PI).
Alongside the first theme – or more accurately, wrapped
round it as a vine about a tree – is the other, not comfortably
consistent theme, a relativistic one which undermines the
claims constituting the first theme. After stating each theme
I discuss the tension between them, suggest the best way out
of it, and indicate how OC itself, and materials from PI,
affords Wittgenstein's own different basis – a fudged one –
for resolving the tension.

Wittgenstein's conceptions of doubt, certainty and knowledge, his persistent conflation throughout OC of contingent

propositions with those he identifies as 'grammatical' propositions, and his revealing conflation of scepticism with idealism, are central to understanding the themes of OC, and I discuss them in their due places, concluding with an overall evaluation.

My exegetical task is effected by suitably anatomizing OC. The view that I shall call OC1 and which constitutes a version of a foundationalist refutation of scepticism, and therefore a contribution to the theory of knowledge, has two components, the first of which is that scepticism is answered by appeal to the fact that beliefs inhere in a system, and the second of which is that this system of beliefs rests on foundations which give those beliefs their content.[2] Here are some passages exemplifying the first component of OC1 (all emphases are Wittgenstein's):

---

2   The first component is paradigmatically expressed in paragraphs 3, 24, 54, 56 (WR248), 57, 82, 83 (WR249), 87–92, 94, 95, 102, 103, 105, 114, 136, 138, 140, 146, 151, 162 (WR252), 209 (WR254), 219, 246, 271, 310–15, 341, 410–11, 457, 494, 512, 517–18. The second component is paradigmatically expressed in paragraphs 35–6 (WR247), 83 (WR249), 103, 105, 136, 151, 162 (WR252), 211 (WR254), 246–53 (WR256–8) (esp. 248), 296, 378, 380–1 and 384–5, 401, 403, 411, 440, 449, 494, 496, 512, 514, 519, 524, 558, 599, 614, 670.

83. The *truth* of certain empirical propositions belongs to our frame of reference (WR249).

88. It may be for example that *all enquiry on our part* is set so as to exempt certain propositions from doubt, if they are ever formulated.

94. But I did not get my picture of the world by satisfying myself of its correctness; nor do I have it because I am satisfied of its correctness. No: it is the inherited background against which I distinguish between true and false.

105. All testing, all confirmation and disconfirmation of a hypothesis takes place already within a system . . . The system is not so much the point of departure, as the element in which our arguments have their life.

162. I have a world picture. Is it true or false? Above all it is the substratum of all my enquiring and asserting (WR252).

341. The *questions* that we raise and our *doubts* depend on the fact that some propositions are exempt from doubt, are as it were like hinges upon which those turn.

Here are some passages exemplary of the second component of OC1:

> 103. And now if I were to say 'It is my unshakeable conviction that etc.', this means in the present case too that I have not consciously arrived at the conviction by following a particular line of thought, but that it is anchored in all my *questions and answers*, so anchored that I cannot touch it.

> 162. I have a world picture. Is it true or false? Above all it is the substratum of all my enquiring and asserting (WR252).

> 411. If I say '*we assume* that the earth has existed for many years past' (or something similar), then of course it sounds strange that we should *assume* such a thing. But in the entire system of our language-games it belongs to the foundations. The assumption, one might say, forms the basis of action, and therefore, naturally, of thought.

> 512. Isn't the question this: 'What if you had to change your opinion even on these most fundamental things?' And to that the answer seems to me to be: 'You don't *have* to change. That is just what their being "fundamental" is.'

599. To say: in the end we can only adduce such grounds as *we* hold to be grounds, is to say nothing at all.

OC1 thus states that scepticism gets no purchase because our beliefs inhere in a system (the first component) which rests upon foundations (the second component), which latter non-negotiably constitute the conditions upon which our beliefs have content – and which therefore constitute the conditions even for doubting, which, therefore again, cannot take the foundations for their target. The justification for the foundations is thus effected by a 'transcendental argument':[3] restated, it is that foundational beliefs (expressed by what Wittgenstein calls, in senses of 'logical' and 'grammatical' special to OC, logical or grammatical propositions; see e.g. 51, 56–8) are what make the system possible, and it is within the system that claims to knowledge and challenges of doubt are alone intelligible. A clever encapsulation of the transcendental argument is given at 248: 'I have arrived at the rock-

---

3   A transcendental argument is one which identifies the conditions under which something is possible; at its simplest, its structure is: X cannot be the case unless Y is the case; therefore, given that X is indeed the case, Y is the case too. See A. C. Grayling, 'Transcendental Arguments', in J. Dancy and E. Sosa (eds), *The Blackwell Companion to Epistemology*, Blackwell, 1992, and Chapter 3 above.

bottom of my convictions. And one might almost say that these foundation-walls are carried by the whole house.'

The view I shall call OC2 and which is not comfortably consistent with – perhaps, indeed, undermines – OC1, is to be found in paragraphs 65, 95–9, 166, 174, 192, 211 (WR254), 253, 256 (WR257–8), 307, 336 (and compare 559) – and perhaps also in paragraphs 5, 33, and 607. Here are some exemplary passages:

65. When language-games change, then there is a change in concepts, and with the concepts the meanings of words change.

95. The propositions describing this world-picture might be part of a kind of mythology . . .

97. The mythology may change back into a state of flux, the river-bed of thoughts may shift.

99. And the bank of the river consists partly of hard rock, subject to no alteration or only to an imperceptible one, partly of sand, which now in one place now in another gets washed away, or deposited.

166. The difficulty is to realise the groundlessness of our believing.

256. On the other hand a language-game does change with time.

336. But what men consider reasonable or unreasonable alters.

OC2 is relativism. Relativism is the view that truth and knowledge are not absolute or invariable, but dependent upon viewpoint, circumstances or historical conditions. What is true for me might not be true for you; what counts as knowledge from one viewpoint might not do so from another; what is true at one time is false at another. Paragraph 97 arguably shows that the relativism implicit in this aspect of OC is of a classic or standard type. Its presence in OC is entirely consistent with its presence elsewhere in the later writings: one remembers the lions and Chinese of PI. What was left open in those earlier relativistic remarks was the degree of strength of the relativism to which Wittgenstein was committed. OC2 constitutes a claim that the framework within which claims to knowledge and challenges of doubt equally make sense is such that its change can reverse what counted as either. *That* is classically strong relativism.

To get a good feel for the tension between OC1 and OC2, compare 103 (where a given belief 'is anchored in all my *questions and answers*, so anchored that I cannot shake it') with 97–9 ('the river-bed of thoughts may shift'); 494 with 256; both 512 and 517 with any of the relativistic remarks cited, for example 559; and any of the relativistic remarks with 317 and 599, which latter is worth repeating here: 'To say: in the end we can only adduce such grounds as *we* hold to be grounds, is to say nothing at all.'

At one level, OC1 and OC2 can of course be so interpreted as to make them consistent. One can postulate foundations that are historically and in other ways parochial to the discourse under consideration, consisting in beliefs and principles which are basic in the OC1 sense for a given discourse, and not justified independently of it; but which are not immutable or absolute but as vulnerable to change, even if more slowly and circumstantially, as any of the ordinary beliefs comprehended in the framework. This precisely seems to be the import of Wittgenstein's river-bed metaphor: the river bed is only *relatively* stable with respect to the water flowing over it, because it is worn away with time, and shifts its course.

But a relativistic foundationalism renders OC1 superficial as a response to scepticism, because so construed it does not begin to meet the *really* serious problem that scepticism poses, and of which Wittgenstein is perfectly aware (see, e.g., 14–16). To see what that is, one must retrace some steps.

Let us simplify the model we are working with. A sceptic challenges us to justify a particular empirical belief, for example that there is a book on the table here before us. We respond, exploiting the same resource for doing so as OC does, by saying in effect that these circumstances are such and those words mean such that this is tantamount to a paradigmatic circumstance for using those words in these circumstances – that is, for claiming that there is a book on the table. The sceptic pushes his point, invoking considerations about non-standard perceptual phenomena and other psychological contingencies, including error; at which point we change gear and invoke countervailing considerations about the framework of the discourse (the system of beliefs constituting it; the 'conceptual scheme') by stating the assumptions upon which not just the claim, but also the challenge to it, make sense. And at this level of sceptical challenge, that has to be enough: justifications in ordinary discourse come to an end at this point.

But *now* the sceptic mutates; he becomes a different and bigger monster. He is no longer interested in hearing what we have to say about the book on the table, but in what we have to say about the framework, the system of beliefs. What justifies our acceptance of the framework, or (more weakly) our employment of it? What if there were another framework, or other frameworks, in which different assumptions led to different outcomes with these words and these circumstances? And so on. The sceptic, in other words, has adopted the habiliments of relativism. Relativism, indeed, is the ultimate form of scepticism, because it challenges us to justify, as a whole, the scheme within which mundane judgements get their content and have their life.

The answer which says: 'This is the scheme we have; it is a

bare given that we have it', and which might – but this is a different thing – add, 'and of course there might be others', and – yet a further and a bigger step again – 'we might never know what these other schemes are like or even that they exist', is unsatisfactory, at very least as the first response to relativism. One might *end* by responding with (in this emergency: preferably) the first step just described, after a long haul; but there are strong anti-relativist arguments to evaluate first, which, if they turn out to be plausible and stable in the face of challenge, provide a powerful way of blocking scepticism altogether. It would seem that for the argument of OC1 to work as a refutation of scepticism, this stronger recourse is required. Without it, knowledge and truth are concepts parochial to the scheme; they are not *knowledge* and *truth* but 'knowledge-in-the scheme' and 'truth-in-the scheme', as 599 says. (Think of being told that '"Jarndyce is a lawyer" is true "in" *Bleak House*' is the *only kind* of exemplification the concept of truth has.)

There are good reasons for thinking that the assumptions constitutive of the framework have to be undischargeable. These reasons are drawn from seeing how the notion of *alternative frameworks* collapses under direct pressure, the terminus of the argument being that anything recognizable as a framework has to be identical in fundamental respects with the framework from which it is so recognized. The argument is adapted from a familiar one offered by Davidson, who writes of 'conceptual schemes' rather than frameworks, and individuates them as sets of intertranslatable languages.[4]

The argument, familiarly enough, is as follows. The relativist proposal is that there can be languages which we might not be able to recognize as such – which, that is, we cannot translate. But how do you recognize a language as such if you cannot translate it? The problem can be stated in terms of what the only plausible candidate for a criterion of languagehood can be: namely, translatability into a familiar idiom. Since language-use involves 'a multitude of finely discriminated intentions and beliefs' which we could not attribute to someone unless we could understand his speech, we can only recognize the presence of such intentions and beliefs if translation is possible. Moreover, if it turns out that there are differences between our and the alien's beliefs, this will be courtesy of a shared background of beliefs which makes the differences apparent. Differences are more meaningful when there are fewer of them; when there are few against a shared background of belief, the differences are more of opinion than conceptualization – they relate to variances in the scheme's superstructure, which tolerates conflicts of view in (for characteristic examples) politics and taste, while still locating them in the same world. Since the cognitive foundations of the scheme

---

4   D. Davidson, 'On the Very Idea of a Conceptual Scheme', *Inquiries into Truth and Interpretation*, Oxford University Press, 1984, pp. 183–98.

have to be shared for these more entertaining differences to be possible, the conclusion is that conceptual relativism is incoherent. (Davidson takes this to mean that the very idea of a framework is empty because it implies what the argument denies: namely, the possibility of real conceptual diversity.)

Underlying such arguments, *very* interestingly, is an implicit commitment to the controversial view that possibility is an epistemic notion; that is, that possibility is conceivability.[5] Something is a possible state of affairs (a possible past fact, a possible language or scheme) only if it is constructible from actual states of affairs (from what we know, from the language we speak). The intended contrast is this: on the idea that possibility is a purely logical notion, denoting mere absence of contradiction, the number of possible worlds there can be other than the actual world is infinite. But on the idea that possibility is an epistemic notion, denoting graspability in thought (or translatability into a familiar idiom), the number of possible worlds other than the actual world is limited by accessibility relations between them and it. But

---

5   It is important that conceivability should not be muddled with 'imagineability'. To conceive is to form and apply concepts, under whatever constraints are required for the concepts to have content. A model set of constraints in the empirical canon could be derived from this loosely specified condition: for a concept to have content it must be derived from and/or have application to experience. Cf. my *Berkeley: The Central Arguments*, Duckworth, 1986, pp. 28–40.

where there are such relations, the idea of a world being in some strong sense different from this one loses its grip. Standard ways of defining possible worlds involve redistributing truth-values over the propositions constituting the world-book of the actual, or increasing their number by adding other propositions consistent with them. But to do this is to redescribe this world, not – except by courtesy of the phrase – to create new worlds.

These considerations rule out relativism. They therefore rule out OC2. There is no other way of taking OC2 than as a seriously strong relativist argument ('the river-bed of thoughts may shift' . . . 'a language-game changes with time'). In the ideal state of things, therefore, OC1's offer of a response to scepticism is elected to stand, and OC2 is ditched. But as the text of OC was left to us, Wittgenstein was developing arguments for both, so the next question is: is there any way they could be made to reconcile, further up the road where their parallels meet?

The destination available to Wittgenstein in the light of the tension between OC1's need for an anti-relativistic resource, and OC2's undermining of this, is one made familiar by his treatment of the request for justifications in PI. It is to say: justification must come to an end: 'My spade is turned'. In PI this seemed to offer a form of foundationalism in which the basis – the given, that which justifies itself by being what it is – is *practice*: and moreover shared practice, which in its essentially mutual character is constitutive of the content (so, in the case of language, the meaning) of what is based upon it. This indeed is Wittgenstein's resource: see 7, 92, 110, 116, 196 (WR253), 229, 559; and perhaps also 232, 219, 344 and 378. Does this do, as a somewhat fudging way out of the problem?

I think not, because the PI turned-spade thesis is considerably weakened in OC by the degree of relativism OC2 constitutes. Of course there are relativistic noises in PI: such claims as that we would not understand a speaking lion if we met one, and that we no more understand Chinese facial expressions than words, have that tendency, because they are premised on the lack of the shared form of life which makes understanding possible. But *these* relativities could be reducible – nothing implies that we cannot gain entry to the alien forms of life; that is, that we can find ways of translating lionese remarks and Chinese expressions upon doing so. Reducible synchronic relativities look very like familiar cultural differences, and hence are *superficially* relative only.[6] But the idea that the foundations of sense are themselves merely relative – that the bed and banks are in constant process of erosion – implies a greater insecurity. Consider a relativist thesis like Feyerabend's, say, in

---

6   I discuss this at some length in my *Wittgenstein*, Oxford University Press, 1988, pp 104–9. During the writing of those pages I had a long discussion with Norman Malcolm in his Hampstead flat about the lion and Chinese remarks in PI. Malcolm did not think they prompted *any* questions about relativism.

which change in assertion-conditions entails change of sense. A different way of calibrating thermometers on his view changes the meaning of 'temperature'. If the bed and banks of discourse were shifting over time, meanings would change with them. But we would be in the position of a speech community whose meanings are shifting without our realizing the fact, because agreements remain. (The rules change, but we all keep observing them in common as they do so. This falls foul of Wittgenstein's own rule-following considerations. The whole community is in the dilemma of the solitary would-be language user, who cannot tell the difference between following the *same* rule again, and only thinking he is doing so.)

A different and better way out of the problem is to suppose that Wittgenstein might have developed his conflicting lines to the point where the conflict became intolerable – I would say: where he recognized the unhealthy mixing of contingent and framework propositions in his examples, which constantly seduced him into thinking relativistically: more on this shortly. And then he just might have preferred the strong anti-relativist argument available in the line he was himself taking in OC1 on the grounds of sense. For in that aspect of his discussion he in effect reinvented the strategy, as noted, of employing a transcendental argument to show that sceptical challenge is defeated by appeals to the framework. Why not therefore see that the transcendental argument militates equally against relativism?

But if one does not supplement the response to scepticism (OC1) by some such strategy, the exercise in OC is at best partial, at worst self-defeating, with the self-defeat stemming from acceptance of OC2. As OC stands, it stands defeated in just this way, for it only deals with scepticism at the lower, less threatening level, and fails to recognize that scepticism in its strongest form is, precisely, relativism.

There are hints in OC of an alternative better way out: namely, some version of naturalism – in Hume's, not Quine's, sense; that is, as appealing to natural facts about our psychological make-up (not, as in Quine, as appealing to the deliverances of current theory in natural science: although the latter form of naturalism takes itself to absorb the former). See 287: 'The squirrel does not infer by induction that it is going to need stores next winter as well.' This hint is strengthened by 505: 'It is always by favour of Nature that one knows something' and the paradigmatically Humean 277: 'I can't help believing . . .' If one re-reads the practice-cum-form-of-life entries in the light of these – a twist of the kaleidoscope – a plausibly naturalistic thesis comes fully into view.

Strawson brackets Wittgenstein with Hume as a naturalist because of 'resemblances, even echoes' in OC, but says that Wittgenstein does not make 'explicit appeal to Nature'.[7] As we have just seen, this is not so; the appeal is explicit

---

7   P. F. Strawson, *Scepticism and Naturalism: Some Varieties*, Columbia University Press, 1985, p. 14.

enough. Strawson goes on to cite passages constituting the foundationalist component of OC1 as 'echoes' of naturalism.[8] I think one should keep these two -isms clearly apart; they are not the same thing, and do not entail each other. The naturalistic streak in OC is not as strong as Strawson claims; it is a mere echo indeed, much muffled, as things stand, by OC2. But it suggests a genuine alternative, suitably worked up, as a way of protecting OC1 from OC2.

What explains Wittgenstein's inability to shake off OC2-type views is his muddling together contingent or empirical propositions with those he calls 'grammatical propositions' – see, for example, 57, 58, 136: Wittgenstein somewhat vaguely describes these latter as propositions which have the 'peculiar logical role' of fixing the framework – giving the meaning, setting the conditions of intelligibility – for ordinary discourse; they cannot be called into doubt without thereby impugning the whole discourse for which they stand as foundational. This is the fatal flaw that generates the OC1–OC2 conflict. It is simply demonstrated: inspect 93–4, 106–11, 128–9, 143, 159, 167, 234, 273–4, 449, 505, and 614. Here are examples:

> 93. Everything that I have seen or heard gives me the conviction that no man has ever been far from the

---

8   Strawson, *Scepticism*, p. 15.

earth. Nothing in my picture of the world speaks in favour of the opposite.

106. If now the child insists, saying perhaps there is a way of getting [to the moon] which I don't know, etc. what reply could I make to him? . . . But a child will not ordinarily stick to such a belief and will soon be convinced by what we tell him seriously.

234. I believe that I have forebears, and that every human being has them. I believe that there are various cities, and, quite generally, in the main facts of geography and history. I believe that the earth is a body on whose surface we move and that it no more suddenly disappears or the like than any other solid body . . . If I wanted to doubt the existence of the earth long before my birth, I should have to doubt all sorts of things that stand fast for me (WR255).

These are offered as examples of beliefs 'standing fast', but one notices that in 93 and 106 the beliefs mentioned are contingent (true when Wittgenstein wrote them, but false if uttered now), while in 234 grammatical beliefs (everyone has forebears) and contingent ones (there are cities) are mixed together indiscriminately. There are examples of what might uncontroversially be called foundational beliefs – ('there are physical objects', 51) – and when Wittgenstein addresses the problem at 318–23 ('But there is no sharp boundary between methodological propositions and propositions within a method' 318, and see 319) he does not resolve it, but turns directly to a claim about rationality that forms part of his positive account of knowledge, as if, whether or not a proposition is grammatical or contingent, its sense-giving foundational role is conferred on it by its being what 'the reasonable man believes' (323).

The rationality view is, indeed, unexceptionable, in having it that one of the marks of systematic propositions is the epistemically normative authority they exercise. Both grammatical and contingent propositions can be systematic in this way, for among the latter there can be propositions of a high degree of generality which key given areas of discourse, the sense of which presupposes the truth of the proposition: and the proposition is contingent. One can pluck from history examples of such propositions which have since been shown false, with the consequent withering of the discourse, as if its artery had been pinched closed.

But such propositions are not transcendental or grammatical. They are scepticism-rebutting only with respect to challenges to the less general propositions which assume them, and themselves lie open to sceptical challenge of that same internal variety. Their defence against it is supposed to rest on appeal to the system they belong to; that is, to *genuinely* grammatical propositions. But Wittgenstein at times accords them a status indistinguishable from genuinely grammatical propositions; at 136, for example, he speaks of 'a lot of empirical propositions which we affirm without special testing; propositions, that is, which have a peculiar logical role in the system of our empirical propositions'. The difficulty is clearly apparent here: for these 'special empirical propositions' turn out not to be empirical in the ordinary sense: 'We don't, for example, arrive at any of them as a result of investigation' (138). So they are *a priori*; and therefore to explain the sense in which they are also 'empirical' we must suppose them akin to Kant's synthetic *a priori* propositions. But these latter are transcendental in the way Wittgenstein's grammatical propositions are, when he describes them with more care; and as 318–19 shows, Wittgenstein is alive to the difference. So the problem remains.

I have no brief here to reconcile Wittgenstein's views in this connection; I simply point out the conflation to explain the presence in OC of OC2. The explanation is that if one includes among the foundations of the system propositions which are in fact contingent even if they have *some* kind of special status in their language-games, one is bound to accept that their status might change. Hence OC2; and hence the inconsistency in OC as it stands.

The well-known, and persuasive, central tenet of OC is its view that claims to knowledge only make sense where the possibility of doubt exists. Knowledge and doubt are correlative notions, and both knowledge claims and expressions of doubt get their content from their inherence in a framework of assumptions stable both for claims and challenges to them. We take from this the idea the thought that were matters otherwise we would be disabled from grasping that such-and-such a doubt relates to such-and-such a claim to know – that they compete, so to say, over the same epistemic territory. Knowing and doubting are *internal* to a framework (a language game, a practice), and the framework is its own court of appeal. All this depends on OC1 (and is threatened by OC2).

Many passages in OC urge this view. Among the key paragraphs are 121–3 (WR249), 317, 341–2, 354, 450, 519 and 625. Here are exemplary passages:

354. Doubting and non-doubting behaviour. There is the first only if there is the second.

450. A doubt that doubted everything would not be a doubt.

519. Doubt itself rests only on what is beyond doubt.

I take as key passages those that focus on *doubt* because what Wittgenstein's theory of knowledge responds to, taking its cue from Moore and via him the tradition of debate, is scepticism. He offers the other barrel of the shotgun too, in the long debate he has with himself from 483 until the end on 'I know' ('I know that my name is Ludwig Wittgenstein').

Getting his central tenet from *those* paragraphs requires the complete disentanglement of the contingent and grammatical levels of knowledge, which Wittgenstein here thoroughly mixes; yet the underlying work is already done by the respective components of OC1 described above.

As in Moore and the tradition of debate that sees scepticism as sharpening the point of epistemological concerns, the resolution of the crux about doubt yields the required account of knowledge. The thesis of OC, resting on its principal OC1 theme, is clear (and cogent). Of course it only sketches a *kind* of view; it amounts to recognizing that theories of knowledge like, say, Kant's – framework-invoking theories – are on the right lines. Now one would like to see the hard detail of such a theory.

The role of *certainty* in Wittgenstein's view invites comment. A response sometimes offered to the familiar traditional Cartesian quest in epistemology is to point out that certainty is the wrong goal, because it is a psychological state one can entertain with respect to falsehoods: you can be certain that Red Rum will win next week's Derby, yet lose your shirt. One might accordingly argue that the goal should instead be *knowledge*, so understood that it is definitionally something more than the psychological states (believings) an epistemic subject has to be in as a necessary condition for entering the richer, truth-constrained, relation in which 'knowing' consists. However: Moore followed his predecessors in the Cartesian tradition by seeking to forge a connection between enjoying, as an epistemic subject, a particular kind of certainty, with the unsustainability of scepticism about what that attitude addresses. One can make 'being certain' the criterion of knowledge when the proposition one is certain of is entertained as such *without option*; that is, at risk of incoherence or loss of meaning. Wittgenstein, in his turn, follows Moore in adopting this strategy, but offers a deeper explanation of why there is no option: he in effect plays Kant to Moore's Hume.

Consider 8, 30, 42, 193, 194, 308. Wittgenstein acknowledges the difference between knowing and being certain, and offers an account of why the latter is sufficient for the former in the optionless cases: namely, that the certainty is (not identical to, but) a function of indubitability, which in turn is a function of the framework. Certainty is not identical with indubitability because it is a psychological state, whereas indubitability is a property of sense-constituting propositions of a definable class, *viz.* the grammatical propositions.

Note that Wittgenstein's apparent inability to hold apart genuinely grammatical and contingent propositions destabilizes this thesis too, for *relative* indubitability will not do for certainty, as the remarks in the cited paragraphs clearly show. So this is indeed an aspect of OC in need of housekeeping.

Is there a lost opportunity in OC? Its argument is rooted in the same intuitions as the private language argument and its related rule-following considerations, in rejecting the

'I'-perspective of the Cartesian tradition, accepted without question or even awareness by Moore, in which the quest is for *radical* agent-certainty, without a backdrop of publicity constraints on the articulation of thoughts, and arguing in its place for a perspective which admits its debts to a 'we' perspective, in which, that is, the speaking and knowing agent is indebted for his capacities in these respects to the resources of an epistemic–linguistic community (see 440). But this makes it all the more striking that Wittgenstein does not use the private language argument against scepticism, for this argument at very least suggests that the existence of a public realm of referents is a condition of the existence of language, and hence of sceptical doubt itself being articulated. And this goes precisely in the direction he sought.

Apart from the vitiation of Wittgenstein's thesis threatened by OC2, there are other difficulties in OC, of which I here mention one: his conflation of scepticism with idealism. It is not fatal to the OC1-based account of knowledge, but that account needs to be shrived of it.

Wittgenstein identifies scepticism with idealism in 19, 24 and 37 (WR247). In 37, moreover, he shows that he takes realism to be the thesis opposed to idealism. This is an error which many besides Wittgenstein make. Realism and idealism are not opposed theses; they are not competitors for the same territory, for realism is an epistemological thesis and idealism a metaphysical one. There is no entailment from the truth of either to the negation of the other. Moreover, the chief varieties of idealism are intended to show that, in an associated epistemological sphere, scepticism gets no grip. Consider Berkeley; it was the avowed aim of his construction of an anti-realist epistemology and (what is a different and further matter) idealist metaphysics, to refute scepticism.[9]

Idealisms form a various family of theses about the nature of reality, but it is safe to say that their characteristic common thesis is the metaphysical one that the universe is mental. Their chief historical opponent is materialism, the metaphysical thesis that the universe is material; that is, ultimately consists of 'material substance', a view that should not be confused with physicalism, which claims that the universe consists of what can be described by physics. (What can be described by physics is not only not coterminous with matter, but might well entail that there is no such thing as matter.)

Idealism is not the same thing as anti-realism. This latter is an epistemological thesis which denies that the relations between thought and its objects, perception and its targets, experience and the realms over which it ranges (these are different, though related, relations) are external or contingent relations. There are realistic forms of idealism (see, for example, Sprigge),[10] and there is no reason in principle why

---

9   Cf. A. C. Grayling, *Berkeley*, op. cit.
10 T. L. S. Sprigge, *The Vindication of Absolute Idealism*, Edinburgh University Press, 1983.

there should not be anti-realistic forms of materialism or – even more plausibly – physicalism. I take it that quantum theory under the Copenhagen interpretation is an anti-realist physicalism.

The claim that the relations between thought and its objects (etc.) is internal is far from the claim that all objects of thought are *causally dependent* upon thought (or, more generally, experience, or sentience) for their existence. Certain forms of idealism (for example, Berkeley's) put matters this way, and doubtless this is why some confuse idealism with anti-realism. Rather, anti-realism is at most the claim – until more is said; as to which, there can be much variety – that no complete description of either relatum can leave out mention of the other.

It is important to be clear about what this means. Realism is the view that the relation between thought and its objects is contingent or external, in the sense that description of neither relatum essentially involves reference to the other. This is the force of saying that realism asserts the independence of things from any mental or perceptual acts that might intend them. Call this the 'independence thesis'. Anti-realists argue that this thesis is incoherent. A simple way of showing why is afforded by the idiom of relations already adopted. A little reflection shows that the independence thesis, understood as the claim that the relations between thought and its objects are external, is a mistake at least for the direction object-to-thought, for any account of the content of thoughts about things, and in particular the individuation of thoughts about things, essentially involves reference to the things thought about – this is given by the least that can be said in favour of notions of 'broad content'. So realism offers us a peculiarly hybrid relation: external in the direction thought-to-things, internal in the direction things-to-thought. It is an easy step for the anti-realist to show that thought about (perception of, theories of) things is always and inescapably present in, and therefore conditions, any full account of the things thought about. The poorly worded 'Tree Argument' in Berkeley, aimed at showing that one cannot conceive of an unconceived thing, is aimed at making just that elementary point.[11] The best statement of such a view is afforded by the Copenhagen interpretation of quantum theory alluded to, in which descriptions of quantum phenomena are taken *essentially* to involve reference to observers and conditions of observation. Such a view does not constitute a claim that the phenomena are *caused* by observations of them. No more does anti-realism claim this. However, a moment's thought shows that if this claim – that the relations between thought and things is internal – is correct, then one needs to think again about truth, objectivity, the modalities and knowledge.[12]

11 Berkeley, *Principles*, para. 23; and Grayling, *Berkeley*, pp. 113–17.
12 See A. C. Grayling, *The Question of Realism*, Oxford, forthcoming.

One often sees an opposition posed between realism and idealism, as if the labels marked competitors for the same terrain. As the foregoing shows, this is a surprisingly common, simple, but serious mistake.

Wittgenstein makes this mistake. But he also makes the mistake, or seems to, of confusing idealism and scepticism. This mistake stems from the crude view that idealism consists in the denial of the existence of the external world, and that this is what scepticism denies too. But as we see, idealism is the metaphysical claim that the world is ultimately mental in some sense, and scepticism is an epistemological challenge to us to justify our beliefs and our methods of acquiring them. In view of this, one is sometimes puzzled as to what exactly Wittgenstein takes scepticism to be. It has already been noted that he confuses the 'grammatical' and the contingent as targets of sceptical attack; here he seems to imply that a sceptic *claims* something (*viz.* that the world is ideal). But it is obvious that scepticism had better not be an agniology. The scepticism that consists in challenges to justify our beliefs and epistemic practices, rather than claims that (weakly) we lack or (more strongly) cannot have knowledge in some domain, is the scepticism most worth addressing.

Strip away all but OC1 as characterized at the outset, and it can be seen as addressing scepticism thus conceived. So protection of the central insight of OC is possible: it requires no more than selective pressure on the 'delete' key.

OC is uncharacteristic of Wittgenstein in at least one striking way: that it is straightforward workaday philosophy of just the kind he earlier thought his views demonstrated to be fly-in-the-bottle. Perhaps this is evidence of a third turn; had Wittgenstein lived we might have seen him engaging even more with the problems of the philosophical tradition, thus tracing a journey from, first, thinking he had solved all its problems, to, second, articulating a different vision of how we misunderstand the workings of our language and thereby generate spurious problems, to, third and finally, seeing that philosophical problems are real ones after all, amenable to investigation – and *solution*.

Wittgenstein makes a contribution to solving the central problem in epistemology in OC. His contribution is to insist on the internal connection between the concepts of knowing and doubting. This is useful to the work of showing that epistemic justification is provided by the conceptual scheme within which it alone gets content. The provisional character of OC leaves much hanging: OC2, the grammar-contingency matter, and the unworked conception of scepticism are examples. One of the most serious of the matters left hanging was recognized by Wittgenstein himself as such: the vague and generalized appeal to practice and a 'form of life' as the basis of the scheme, carried over from PI: 'Now I would like to regard this certainty, not as something akin to hastiness or superficiality, but as a form of life. (That is very badly expressed and probably badly thought as well)' (358). (Read this remark with, for example, 94, 105 and 162 (WR252) open before one.) But even as a provisional and sketchy view OC offers convincing support for a set of possibilities – admittedly, familiar ones – debated elsewhere in the epistemological tradition; namely, the framework-invoking or 'conceptual scheme'-invoking refutation of scepticism.[13]

13 For example, P. F. Strawson, *Individuals*, Routledge, 1959; and Grayling, *Refutation of Scepticism*, 1985.

CHAPTER 5

Naturalistic Assumptions: Quine

Naturalized epistemology is epistemology based on accepting the deliverances of our best current theories about the world, and premising them in the account we give of how we get those theories. One of its principal attractions is that it allows us to make progress with other tasks in philosophy and elsewhere, unhampered by sceptical doubts. The paralyzing effect of self-conscious questions about the getting and testing of beliefs – prompted in the tradition of epistemology by an acute sense of the finitary predicament not just of each putative knower taken individually, but of the collective even as it pools the results of its members' best endeavours – is solved in naturalized epistemology by the simple expedient of avoiding those questions altogether.

But naturalized epistemology has a tendency to make one uneasy. Its attractiveness can come to seem a corner-of-the-eye affair, lasting only while one's gaze is fixed elsewhere.

Under direct scrutiny it appears to have two serious defects, each individually fatal to it, but interestingly linked. These are that it is circular, and that it seems comprehensively to miss the point – or if not, to duck the demand – of traditional epistemology. Without doubt these complaints, in one or another formulation, are wearisomely familiar to naturalism's proponents, but I have yet to see a satisfactory response to them, and so take this opportunity to seek one.

In Quine's view, epistemology naturalized is epistemology treated as part of science – in effect, as an empirical psychological enquiry into how we get our beliefs about nature. In an often-quoted passage from the eponymous paper that launched the debate, Quine writes:

Epistemology, or something like it, simply falls into place as a chapter of psychology and hence of natural science. It studies a natural phenomenon, viz. a physical human subject. This human subject is accorded a certain experimentally controlled input – certain patterns of irradiation in assorted frequencies, for instance – and in the fullness of time the subject delivers as output a description of the three-dimensional external world and its history. The relation between the meagre input and the torrential output is a relation that we are prompted to study for somewhat the same reasons that have always prompted epistemology: namely, in order to see how evidence relates to theory, and in what ways one's theory of nature transcends any available evidence.[1]

On the face of it, naturalization would seem to mark a change of focus as against traditional concerns, bearing out the charge laid by Rorty and others that Quine has substituted a causal enquiry for the justification-seeking one that the label 'epistemology' traditionally denotes. If so, of course, there could be a complaint only about bending the name to a different purpose, a very minor injury to those still interested in justificatory questions, for what's in a name? –

1 'Epistemology Naturalised', *Ontological Relativity and Other Essays*, Columbia University Press, 1969, pp. 82–3. Cf. also: 'Epistemology is best looked upon . . . as an enterprise within natural science. Cartesian doubt is not the way to begin. Retaining our present beliefs about nature, we can still ask how we can have arrived at them. Science tells us that our only source of information about the external world is through the impact of light rays and molecules upon our sensory surfaces. Stimulated in these ways, we somehow evolve an elaborate and useful science. How do we do this, and why does the resulting science work so well? These are genuine questions, and no feigning of doubt is needed to appreciate them. They are scientific questions about a species of primates, and they are open to investigation in natural science, the very science whose acquisition is being investigated': 'The Nature of Natural Knowledge', in S. Guttenplan, *Mind and Language*, Oxford University Press, 1975.

they could continue their task and call it 'Fred'. But Quine insists that there has been no change of subject matter; naturalized epistemology is truly epistemology; what it does is to improve on the traditional variety. Like the traditional variety, it tackles the question of the relation of evidence to theory; but it is epistemology grown up, explaining the relation of sensory inputs to outputs of theory on the basis of empirically checkable facts about how we learn to speak of the world. It transpires that *learning to speak* is the epistemic crux for Quine, for doing so, as he puts it, 'virtually enacts the evidential relation'; and he has a psychogenetic account that sketches how.[2] It follows that epistemology is no longer 'first philosophy' in the Cartesian sense, because there is no magisterial justificatory task for it to perform. Insofar as justification is to the point at all – and it is not – it comes tangentially and free, because it comes pragmatically; total theory works, which is all that needs to be said. (I speak here of course of justification as it would be sought by what Quine asperses as a 'supra-scientific tribunal'; namely, traditional epistemology. There is an internal, naturalized sense of justification, the getting of evidence for theories by observation and hypothetico-deductive reasoning which science itself, in the form of psychology, teaches us: but by 'justification' in

2   'The Nature of Natural Knowledge', pp. 74–5; see also *The Roots of Reference*, Open Court, 1974, p. 3.

all of what follows I shall mean the ambitious variety of traditional epistemology.)

One of Quine's main motives for supplanting traditional with naturalized epistemology is that, in his view, the former attempted to get science from sensings by a reductionist project after the various manners of Hume, Russell in one of his phases, and Carnap – who is Quine's principal target in this connection. Quine famously rejects the reductionism involved, but accepts that epistemology 'contains' science in the sense that science is indeed projected from data, as the output consequent to sensation. But the containment in that direction is reciprocal to a containment in the other: science contains epistemology, because epistemology is part of psychology. The reciprocity has the effect that epistemology itself turns out to be, like the rest of science, 'our own construction or projection from stimulations'.[3]

It is this 'reciprocity' that looks squarely circular (so to speak). Quine recognizes this, but argues that giving up the dream of deducing science from sense data breaks the circle, or perhaps renders it virtuous. If the enterprise of effecting a reductive translation of physical language into sense datum language cannot be carried through, then the Janus face of psychology begs no questions in looking both ways.

What is the objection to this? Well, it is that Quine has taken it that the one alternative to naturalized epistemology –

---

3   See *Roots*, p. 83.

that is, psychology – is epistemology which involves reductive translation. His immediate target is Carnap's 'rational reconstruction', but this can serve to represent phenomenalisms in general, since it shares with them an ambition to exhaust external-world talk in experiential talk without remainder. But why should such a strategy be thought the only alternative to naturalized epistemology? And why should it be thought that rejecting it disposes of any interest in justification?

Let us note how Quine comes to think that the reductivist project is naturalism's only alternative. He starts by stating that epistemology is concerned with the foundations of science, which includes mathematics. In just the way that study of mathematics neatly divides into 'conceptual' and 'doctrinal' studies – that is, investigations respectively into meaning and truth – so too does the study of natural knowledge. On the conceptual side, the task is to show how natural knowledge is based on sense experience. On the doctrinal side, the task is to justify natural knowledge in sensory terms. In Quine's view the doctrinal side fails; we have not, he says, advanced beyond Hume's despair on this head. But on the conceptual side there has been progress, made possible by the technique of contextual definition.

Carnap's 'heroic efforts' to effect a rational reconstruction of natural knowledge in terms of sense experience supplemented by logic and set theory, lie on the conceptual side. If successful, his efforts would identify and clarify the sensory evidence for science, even if they failed to show how its possession *justifies* science; and they would deepen our understanding of our discourse about the world. But they do not succeed, because the reductive translation required does not go through: Quine's argument needs no rehearsing here. Quine therefore writes, 'If all we hope for is a reconstruction that links science to experience in explicit ways short of translation, then it would seem more sensible to settle for psychology.'[4]

Let us grant the point about reductive translation. Quine next assumes that naturalized epistemology and epistemologies that turn on translation between them exhaust the options. But this is just incorrect; there are a number of non-reductive ways for the justificatory enterprise to proceed. Take just one example: a remarkable feature of Quine's claim about the foundering of the doctrinal project in Hume is his neglect of what that failure immediately prompted; namely, Kant's critical enterprise, and what that directly or indirectly prompted in its turn; namely, the possibilities it suggested to some – Strawson and the very late Wittgenstein, in not very different ways, included – for exploiting more forensic conceptions of justification than is envisaged by austere versions of empiricism taken alone.[5] It is not necessary to dilate on

---

4   *Roots*, p. 78.
5   'Forensic': Kant saw the question of justification on analogy with legal justification: in effect, as an establishing of right or entitlement to given beliefs. It might seem implausible to assign Wittgenstein a place in the Kantian tradition, but it is not too far from the point; he had after all been much influenced by

these options here; we have merely to be reminded of their existence to see that we are not faced with a simple disjunctive syllogism. If naturalized epistemology is to rest to any degree on ruling out the opposition, it will have to show that all other approaches to the doctrinal task founder too.

Quine resisted the charge of circularity, recall, by saying that so long as investigation of the evidential link between sense data and theory is not regarded as addressing questions about justification, no circle is at stake. He assumed that the attempt to secure justification consists in the attempt to reduce theory to data, and so could argue that abandoning hopes of a translation amounts to abandoning the justificatory enterprise. If so, the circle breaks, or turns virtuous: where there is no attempt at justification, it begs no questions to premises in epistemology what traditional epistemology took itself as having to justify. But the foregoing remarks show that so far we have not been shown that the justificatory enterprise is bankrupt, because we are not bound to identify it with the reductionism that Quine rejects.

The next step in showing that naturalism does not escape circularity is to demonstrate something stronger; namely, that the justificatory question is anyway unavoidable. Quine says that epistemology is concerned with the foundations of science. A concern with the foundations of science – a foun-

Schopenhauer, and *On Certainty* has its antecedents in the *Tractatus*.

dational concern – sounds like a concern with assumptions, aims, ontology, methodology and reasoning, one of the chief points in investigating all which – if not *the* chief point – is to ascertain how to tell good theories from bad. This is much more than just seeking to understand the links between evidence and theory, where such understanding falls short of providing justifications. We wish to know when the links are strong enough to bet one's money or one's life on them. We recognize that there are different kinds of evidential relations, individuated by subject matter. We wish to control what can count as evidence for a given subject matter, and to know when caution (or to call it otherwise: doubt) is appropriate, and what can legitimately prompt it. Most of our concerns – in the physician's consulting room, on the construction site, in the pharmaceutical laboratory, on the battlefield – are austerely practical ones, where reliable means of forming judgements are at a premium. We therefore have to try to advance beyond merely *understanding* evidential links where doing so falls short of showing how they bestow a licence to rely on certain of them, for such understanding must be the basis for yielding something more: namely, norms. A conception of 'getting it right' in a given area of endeavour matters to us; and it demands tests and a way of recognizing when they have been passed or failed. Hence, the justificatory enterprise is a non-negotiable part of epistemology. It is why epistemology got started.

So that there is no chance of misunderstanding what is at

stake here, allow me to iterate. Quine describes the enterprise of naturalized epistemology as the endeavour (I quote) 'simply to understand the link between observation and science' when he is specifically seeking to avoid the circularity charge. That makes it sound as if the task is a very modest one; the passage in full reads,

> Scruples against circularity have little point once we have stopped dreaming of deducing science from observations. If we are out simply to understand the link between observation and science, we are well advised to use any available information, including that provided by the very science whose link with observation we are trying to understand.[6]

Now as we see, the strongly normative character that we expect to follow from understanding evidential links alters the picture. Getting into possession of epistemic norms neither *has* to, nor *does* amount to, deducing science from observations, but neither is it *just* understanding a non-justificatory connection. So we could entirely eschew the attempt to carry out remainderless translations of talk about the external world into a reducing class of sensation sentences, but the attempt to demonstrate the nature and

---

6   'Epistemology Naturalised', p. 76.

relative strengths of the support provided to theories by observations is a practical necessity, and for this it will not do to premise what is to be tested in an account of what tests them. Given that, the circle on which naturalized epistemology bases itself is vicious.

At this juncture, by way of aside, one might register a concern about the non-justificatory notion of 'evidence' in play here. Standardly, the notion seems intrinsically to be one that exists precisely to play the traditional epistemological role of confirming and infirming, supporting and weakening given claims by its respective presences or absences. In Quine the notion is tied to sensory stimulation, and left otherwise – and explicitly – unexplained: he writes that in his theory 'the term "evidence" gets no explication and plays no role'.[7] This, obviously, is a luxury that can be afforded only when we have given up on doctrinal studies altogether.

The foregoing remarks are based on a *pro tempore* acceptance of Quine's claim that epistemology concerns the foundations of science. But – and here is the second of the two objections to be urged against the naturalizing programme – epistemology is surely concerned with a good deal more than this. It is more even than a concern with science (that is, with the superstructure as well as the foundations of science), unless the word 'science' is stretched to denote with

---

7   'Comment on Davidson', in *Perspectives on Quine*, R. Barrett and R. Gibson (eds), Blackwell, 1990, p. 80.

complete generality everything we hope we know. (It had this meaning in the early modern period.) For there are plenty of things we might hope to know beyond the structure and properties of the material world, which is what the natural sciences deal with. We wish also to know about history, for example, and the motives and feelings of others, and whether there is anything of value in the world, ethically and aesthetically; and we are surely interested in the differences between ways of knowing some of these things and knowing others. And as before, we have our exigent practical concerns, which makes getting things right a vital interest, and poses the demand that traditional epistemology exists precisely as an attempt to satisfy. Even the most hardened non-cognitivist in ethics, for example, must accept that we are good readers of the intentions of our fellows, and although physical entities play their part in this – raised eyebrows, air-waves issuing from mouths – it takes an even more exotic form of reductionism than Quine repudiates in Carnap; namely a belief that in the end everything will be expressible in the language of physics, to think that our other epistemic interests, in history and folk psychology and these other spheres, can be naturalized along with the epistemology of science.

Commitment to physicalist reduction cannot be foisted on Quine, however, because although it is naturalistic, it does not exhaust naturalism. Roger Gibson reminds us that Quine infers from the fallibility of science the view that future science might tell us that there is more to evidence than sensory stimulation, and that therefore adherence to empiricism must be tentative.[8] So naturalism is not to be defined as acceptance of the deliverances of physical theory together with what it tells us about how we get it (that is, by empirical means); it is rather to be defined as acceptance of *current* such theory, for any 'current'. If the theory changes, acceptance must go with it; naturalism lies, in short, in following the fashion. This is integral to naturalistic epistemology's break with justificatory concerns, as witness these facts: a good naturalist in the thirteenth century AD, or the thirteenth century BC, would on his naturalistic principles have been bound to go with the current theory of the day. The dramatic nature of past theory change teaches us that being naturalistic at any point in the history of science is therefore a matter quite independent of whatever justification scientists in different periods have had for their claims, whether about the fifth essence, the pulsative faculty of the heart, phlogiston, or the colour and strangeness of quarks: take your pick.

Naturally we all feel confident that even if quarks go the way of phlogiston, current science has got it much righter than ever before, and in some cases, we suspect, has got it right *simpliciter*, so it at least seems safe to be epistemologically

8   R. Gibson, 'Quine on the Naturalising of Epistemology', in *On Quine: New Essays*, Paolo Leonardi and Marco Santambrogio (eds), Cambridge University Press, 1995, p. 90.

naturalistic *now*. We have our Enlightenment belief in progress and the growth of knowledge – I too find such faith compelling – and some even take this to mean that we are more and more closely approximating the truth of things. But this means we should, in the interests of consistency, brush aside the possibility that our remoter descendants, if we have any, might split their sides over twentieth-century textbooks of physics.

These remarks might independently serve to prompt scepticism about naturalized epistemology, but in connection with the circularity problem they add an emphasis. Naturalism enjoins the premising of *current* theory in explanations of how we come by that theory. To see again why this is deeply unsatisfactory, take a naturalized stand on behalf of our thirteenth-century AD or BC epistemologist, and note how, from that perspective, flat earth and geocentric theories seemed good science in their day. And the fact is, they *are* good science for their day. But that is surely not the point; we wish to know something different; namely, whether they are good science.

In discussing the independence of naturalism from the particular *content* of given current science, Gibson remarks that even if the ontology of current science were to go the way of phlogiston, 'naturalism would persist, for naturalism is not wedded to any particular ontology, for example to physicalism'.[9] Adding this to the claim that future science

9   Gibson, 'Quine', p. 90.

might eject empiricism too – so that theory and method both might go – we get the result that *naturalized epistemology* is immune to the fate of whatever it is itself premised upon at any point in the history of science. This makes it in Popperian terms irrefutable; which in Popperian terms means that it is vacuous.

To see how naturalism misses the point of traditional epistemology – or at least, ducks its demands – we must remind ourselves of what motivates this latter. It is the thought that someone some time has to take a hard look at the familiar, the taken for granted, the apparently indubitable among our beliefs – and sometimes even to challenge some of them. A charming Chinese drawing in the possession of the British Library shows a Qing Dynasty literatus giving his books their annual airing in the spring sunshine; something like this has to be done for our beliefs. Philosophy is where it happens; it is where, among other things, our deepest and most general assumptions come in for their check-ups. In connection with momentous questions about what we believe, and why, and whether we are entitled to, and with what degree of confidence, we cannot assume the very things philosophy should be inspecting. One might put the matter this way: when crossing the street in the path of an oncoming bus, it is advisable to make the usual assumptions about the external world. But the study armchair is not in the path of a bus, and so provides a place apart for thinking about why acceptance of the assumptions is advisable when crossing the street.

The point in epistemology is not to substantiate one or another agniological thesis, which Quine seems to think is threatened by traditional epistemological investigations. Such investigations, familiarly, elicit points of concern: evidence underdetermines theory, theories are defeasible, the ontological status of entities (apparently) referred to by certain theoretical terms is moot, and so forth. Naturalizing epistemology is an attempt to cauterize any haemorrhage of confidence such reflections might provoke. Quine writes that it is a 'peculiarly philosophical fallacy' to 'question the reality of the external world, or deny that there is evidence of external objects in the testimony of our senses, for to do so is simply to dissociate the terms "reality" and "evidence" from the very applications which originally did most to invest those terms with whatever intelligibility they may have for us'.[10] Now this by implication is to suggest that traditional epistemology, with its central positioning of justificatory concerns, leads to just such questioning and denial: but who (Peter Unger and one or two other *provocateurs* apart) ever seriously thought this? Consider Descartes: he is not one jot a sceptic: he is indeed far less of one than a self-respecting naturalized epistemologist should allow himself to be, out of respect for the open-mindedness of science. Descartes makes methodological use of certain sceptical moves adapted from

---

10 'The Scope and Language of Science', in *The Ways of Paradox*, Harvard University Press, 1979, p. 229.

the antique canon in order to illustrate a point. But the motivation is the excellent one of subjecting the nature of justification to as rigorous a scrutiny as possible, which involves considering even outré possibilities of defeasibility and difficulty. Traditional epistemology thus explores ways of taking serious account of worst-case epistemic situations in order to make the best case for knowledge-claims: an interesting, legitimate and consequential enterprise.

The objection always advanced by naturalizers to this characterization of the epistemological task is that it involves boot-strapping, or an attempt to occupy a theoretical vantage point which is not really available. The traditional task takes itself to be a self-reflexively critical endeavour to stand aside, so to speak, and from that position of notional disengagement to bring under review as many of the facts and possibilities of epistemic life as can be mustered, and to make sense of them. It therefore implicitly rejects the premise of the Neurath ship analogy, which is that we are *essentially* context-bound, *strictly* limited in the task of critical self-reflection by the framework we occupy. And it rejects it because it holds that there are indeed imaginative, comparative, speculative, abstracting, formal, critical, debated, assumption-testing opportunities of reflection available to us, by whose means we interpret our world and our practices to ourselves, and by whose means we push at boundaries. One of the chief of these opportunities is philosophy itself, but such forms of thought are to be found in many other pursuits too, from creative literature to theories of the quantum field.

The link between the two objections has already been made. It lies in the naturalizer's refusal to see epistemology as a justificatory enterprise. To sustain this refusal would be to escape the circularity charge, and to give epistemology a new point: the non-justificatory understanding of connections between experience and science. But if epistemology is stubbornly a justificatory enterprise, to naturalize it is to go in a circle and to duck its chief demand.

What is lost by abandoning naturalization? First, one notes that the baby need not go out with the bath water. A refusal to premise current science in one's epistemology is not a refusal to take current science seriously. Like Descartes, we are not sceptics in any but the healthy sense praised by Russell, and our interest lies in extracting the best lessons science has to offer. Sometimes the lesson is that we do not do well in investigating certain phenomena to employ the techniques that were successful with other phenomena. On the naturalistic view, the psychology of perception – even understood as extendible by the finest technology available at the time – seems to provide a model for too much in the way of enquiry.[11] Still, science is its own recommendation as a success, and invites the liveliest epistemological interest. But

---

11 It does not, for example, help in judging the qualities of a poem, say.

that is not the same thing as giving up thinking about it critically.

In the fabric of Quine's philosophy, naturalism is internally connected with holism, realism and the crucial matter of language acquisition with the empiricist theory of meaning it entails. What effect does giving up naturalism have on these other commitments? Gibson has drawn a clear picture, endorsed by Quine, of how the dependencies lie: holism and realism support naturalism, naturalism supports natural science, and natural science supports empiricism.[12] I shall not here consider holism and empiricist theory of meaning, which are too attractive in principle to argue with, although a corollary of Quine's version of the latter gets some comment below. But there is room for unease over realism. It is not clear to me that realism understood as a thesis about the independence from theory of the things we theorize about is either inherently intelligible or – not surprisingly, if the unintelligibility charge is right – consistent with the other two anyway, although longish tales need to be told why. For present purposes the point need only be that in the version espoused by Quine, realism goes if naturalism does; for the following reason.

On Gibson's endorsed account, Quine's realism is 'unregenerate realism', by which he says he means a sort of naive realism glossed and theorized into more sophisticated shape

---

12 Gibson, 'Quine', p. 93.

by naturalistically understood natural science. It consists in the 'archaic natural philosophy' imbibed with mother's milk, extended in the process of actual and epistemic growing up into something deeper and broader. On this view, common sense is continuous with science.[13] 'To disavow the very core of common sense', says Quine, 'to require evidence for that which both the physicist and the man in the street accept as platitudinous, is no laudable perfectionism; it is a pompous confusion, a failure to observe the nice distinction between the baby and the bath water'.[14] Well: for Russell archaic natural philosophy was the metaphysics of the caveman, and the metaphysics of modern man – namely, science – in his view shows common sense to be false. For Berkeley, grass is green in the dark, and the views of Locke and the New Philosophers (as the corpuscularians were called) absurdly controvert common sense (of which Berkeley took himself to be the doughtiest of champions) by proposing that grass is no colour unless seen, that solid objects enclose mainly empty space, and so on. Now it just seems to me that common sense has its place, that particle physics offers models of a world that is pretty unlike the world of common sense, that any decent theory has to save the *endoxa*, as Aristotle required, but it does not have to *be* the *endoxa* and

---

13 W. V. Quine, 'The Scope and Language of Science', *The Ways of Paradox*, pp. 229–30; Gibson, 'Quine', pp. 94–5.

14 Quine, 'The Scope and Language of Science'.

indeed perhaps had better not be; and that anyway, 'archaic natural philosophy' is not as a whole an historical invariant (remember our thirteenth-century AD and BC predecessors) even if part of it – the medium-sized dry goods part, along with its associated ways of talking – is; but it is hardly enough to get science going. In fact 'unregenerate realism' could well do with a bit of regeneration. It is a natural companion for naturalized epistemology, of course, but it is not clear that either gains by association with the other.

Another important feature of the view that presents some difficulties, in unmodified form at least, is the observation sentence-theoretical sentence considerations that go with Quine's language-acquisition story. The difficulty is very familiar, but bears restatement. It is that for the two kinds of sentence to be relevantly distinguishable – as occupying appropriate logical slots with respect to each other – they have to differ enough in kind. Put schematically, observational sentences have to be relevantly untheoretical, theoretical sentences relevantly unobservational. The latter might be granted, but it is a famous stricture on the former that there are no theory-light sentences. This is to be taken seriously as entailing that any sentence counts as an observation sentence only as a high matter of some theory (and on other occasions might well not so count). Now, observation sentences have a crucial place in the economy of naturalized epistemology; they are 'the cornerstone of semantics', fundamental to language learning as what gets it started, and firmest in meaning because they have their own empirical consequences.[15] They therefore play both conceptual and doctrinal roles, in the minimal sense of the latter allowed by naturalism, as stating the (non-justificatory) evidence for theory. If we are attracted by the idea that there are empirical controls on meaning from its roots up, and that this is a fact about language-acquisition which blocks any move to theories of meaning based on transcendent conceptions of truth, then some way has to be found of construing talk of observation sentences that accommodates Neurath's point about them.

I anticipate that what naturalists will most dislike in the foregoing is of course the insistence on the traditional epistemological conception of the justificatory task. And that is as it should be, since it is that – the question that Quine identifies as the doctrinal one – that has been at the centre of the trouble all along. Now I can register one concluding point. In drawing the parallel between conceptual and doctrinal studies in mathematics and those aimed at knowledge of the natural world, Quine exported the meaning-truth pairing from one to the other more or less intact. Early in 'Epistemology Naturalised' he talks of Hume's despair as to 'the justification of our knowledge of truths about nature'. Of *truths*, note; a traditional truth-incorporating notion of knowledge is in play. But this is not as it should be, although

15 'Naturalised Epistemology', p. 89.

it too often was so in the minds of traditional epistemologists. We have no decent notion of truth to serve the turn, and do not need one; indeed, we need nothing which even remotely resembles the familiar realist versions of truth on offer. For 'knowledge' read 'reliable beliefs' and scrap truth; we can get by with *success most of the time*, because that is how we do get by. So the notion of justification in traditional epistemology is not as exigent as it clearly seemed to Quine in his celebrated paper – although it weakens in a different direction from the one he prefers. I offer it as a thought that this misperception of what justification is supposed to yield in traditional epistemology is perhaps what mistakenly made naturalism feel so natural in the first place.

PART III

SCEPTICISM AND JUSTIFICATION

CHAPTER 6

Scepticism and Justification

Despite traditional appearances, scepticism is not well described as doubt or denial, nor is it properly understood without limitation of subject matter. Rather, it is best and most sharply characterized as a motivated challenge, in a specified area of discourse, to the makers of epistemic claims in that discourse. The challenge is to defend the grounds offered in support of those claims so that the concerns embodied in the sceptic's motivation for issuing the challenge will be met. His motivation consists in the battery of familiar sceptical considerations which, in the tradition of debate on these matters, have come to be called sceptical 'arguments'. One of the main points I urge is that this is a misdescription. Unravelling this characterization gives us our anatomy of scepticism.

First, it is a mistake to think of scepticism as consisting in an agniology; that is, a thesis to the effect that we are ignorant either globally or in some region of enquiry. Certain early forms of scepticism (notably the Pyrrhonian) appeared to take this form, but the briefest reflection shows that global agniology is trivially self-defeating (if we know nothing, then we do not know that we know nothing), while local agniologies must themselves consist in positive claims to the effect that we are ignorant in the given sphere, and any positive claim can itself be challenged for its justification. Of course, weak forms of local agniology – which remind us that our knowledge in given regions of enquiry is incomplete, or provisional, and that a healthy attitude of open-minded scrutiny must greet each new claimed advance in them – are perfectly acceptable (and perhaps reflect moderate academic scepticism, advanced in antiquity in opposition to Pyrrhonism on the grounds that life must be lived). But they do not amount to scepticism in the sense important in epistemology; in this guise they amount merely to injunctions to proportion assent to grounds – in short, to be rational.

But not only is scepticism not well described as the thesis that we are ignorant, it is not even well described as an attitude of doubt. Such an attitude would be premised on the view that there is something inherently suspect about our epistemic practices, a presumption which, when it does not verge on being self-defeating after the manner of global agniology, loads the dice against enquiry before it has offered what it can claim in its support. There is a colloquial use of 'sceptic' to denote one who is very hard to persuade even about the most evident matters – a stance that commits the opposite sin to credulity or too ready assent – which this characterization conveys. But there is as little reason to think in advance that knowledge claims are by their nature largely doomed as to think that they are all justified. Our interest lies in separating the wheat from the chaff; and this we expect an examination of properly characterized scepticism to help us do.

It does so when we recognize scepticism in a given domain of enquiry as a motivated challenge to make out the justification offered for epistemic claims made in that domain. The best sceptic does not himself claim anything; he asks for a defence of our justificatory practices in the light of certain important considerations relating to them. These important considerations concern contingencies affecting our ways of getting, testing, employing and reasoning about our beliefs. The contingencies in question are familiar from the traditional epistemological debate: they relate to the nature of perception, the normal human vulnerability to error, and the existence of states of mind – dreaming, hallucinating, being deluded and the like – which can be subjectively indistinguishable from states that we normally take to be appropriate for reliably forming and employing the beliefs in question. By invoking these considerations the sceptic motivates his request to see the support that can be adduced on behalf of claims made in the course of standard epistemic practice. His invocation of them does not support an agniology, nor does it license doubt beyond the reasonable norm in enquiry. If the sceptic's aim were truly to establish doubt or urge denial, adducing these contingent facts about perception, vulnerability to error and the rest, would not succeed in helping him do either without further strong argument to the effect that these knowledge-defeating contingencies are universal, unavoidable, undetectable (and so on), which would be an extremely hard case to make, if only for the reason that it would require of us that we never fully know what we are talking about when we use such expressions as 'knowledge', 'justification', 'truth' and the like.

But putting matters this way also shows that scepticism is not to be rebutted by saying that we should begin with confidence in our standard epistemic practices, and require the sceptic to show special reason why on any given occasion he himself has justification for mounting a challenge. (Such might be the strategy, for example, of a 'relevant alternatives' rebuttal of scepticism.) The point about the contingent facts which the sceptic can adduce is that they illuminate the (at least *prima facie*) defeasibility of our epistemic practices, and thereby show that there is an onus on us to rule defeaters out when we advance knowledge-claims, or at least to accommodate them, in ways which do not derail the project of getting knowledge, or at least well-justified belief.

It is important to see how the traditional sceptical arguments conform to this diagnosis of scepticism as challenge rather than claim. One characteristic pattern of such argument is drawn from a set of considerations about error, delusions and dreams. Another trades on facts about perceptual relativities and the fact that our cognitive capacities pay a constitutive role in the nature of our experience. Empiricist views suffer particular problems from considerations relating to the nature and limitations of perception, and here the pattern is at its clearest. The best current empirical account of perception tells us a highly complex causal story, beginning with impingements by the environment on our sensory surfaces and ending with the full richness of phenomenal experience and its sequelae in thought and memory. How this remarkable transaction occurs is still mysterious to science and philosophy. But occur it does; and the causal complexity of the process appears richly to invite sceptical challenge. From the subject's viewpoint there might be no way of telling the difference between normally and abnormally caused experience.

The pattern is: if one knows that p, then nothing is acting to defeat one's justification to claim knowledge that p. But one can seem to oneself fully entitled to claim to know some p and in fact lack that entitlement, as the foregoing considerations show. An alternative characterization is to say that we can have the best grounds for claiming to know that p, and yet p can be false; the conjunction of the set of propositions asserting the grounds for p with the negation of p is not a contradiction.[1] Employing this latter idiom captures the

---

1   Grayling, *Refutation*, Introduction and chapter 1; and 'Epistemology', in N. Bunnin and E. P. Tsui-James (eds), *Blackwell Companion to Philosophy*, 1996.

underlying logical structure of the defeasibility of epistemic practice, and the contingency of what makes it so. So our claims to knowledge are in need of better grounds than we standardly take ourselves to have. We must, in short, find a way of defeating the defeaters.

One immediate result of grasping the challenge pattern of scepticism as exemplified in these ways is to note that sceptical considerations are not correctly described as 'arguments'. Sceptical mooting of the familiar considerations is much more like Wittgenstein's 'assembling reminders', by itself enough to show that there is work to be done in justification of epistemic practices. And it follows immediately that if sceptical considerations are neither claims of an agniological tendency, nor arguments purporting to establish an agniology or even just enquiry-undermining infective doubt, then obviously it is a mistake to respond to scepticism as if it were either. In particular, it is a mistake to try to respond to sceptical challenge piecemeal, taking each of the considerations a sceptic might adduce one by one and offering a demonstration that it does not unseat the epistemic project – for the considerations adduced by the sceptic have merely maieutic status, and it is a disjunction of them – or any one of them by itself – which prompts the thought that epistemology has positive work to do in support of justification.

The point can be well illustrated by considering (just as an example) Gilbert Ryle's well-known attempt to refute the argument from error by using a 'polar concept' argument in response. There cannot be counterfeit coins, Ryle observed, unless there are genuine ones, nor crooked paths unless there are straight paths, nor tall men unless there are short ones – and so on. Many concepts come in such polarities, a feature of which is that one cannot grasp either pole unless one simultaneously grasps its opposite. Now, 'error' and 'getting it right' are conceptual polarities. If one understands the concept of error, one understands the concept of getting things right. But to understand this latter concept is to be able to apply it. So our very grasp of the concept of error implies that we sometimes get things right.

Ryle assumed that the sceptic is claiming that, for all we know, we might always be in error. Accordingly his argument – that if we understand the concept of error, we sometimes get things right – is aimed at refuting the intelligibility of claiming that we might always be wrong. But of course the sceptic is not claiming this. He is simply asking how, given that we sometimes make mistakes, we can rule out the possibility of being in error on any given occasion of judgement – say, at this present moment.

But the sceptic need not concede the more general claim Ryle makes; namely, that for any conceptual polarity, both poles must be understood, and – further and even more tendentiously – to understand a concept is to know how to apply it, and for it to be applicable is for it to be applied (or to have been applied). This last move is question-begging enough, but so is the claim about conceptual polarities itself.

For the sceptic can readily cite cases of conceptual polarities – 'perfect–imperfect', 'mortal–immortal', 'finite–infinite' – where it is by no means clear that the more exotic poles apply to anything, or even that we really understand them. Taking a term and attaching a negative prefix to it does not guarantee that we have thereby grasped an intelligible concept.

However, like Descartes' 'dreaming argument' or any of the other familiar sceptical considerations, it is not required that they themselves be sustainable or defensible in any specially robust way. They are not claims; they are suggestions, considerations, examples, adduced to motivate the challenge.

These remarks imply that sceptical considerations, even if singly they appear implausible, jointly invite a serious response; which is what, centrally, epistemology seeks to offer.

One reflex way of describing the anti-sceptical task of epistemology is (as both Descartes and Russell formulated it in classic texts[2]) to discover the grounds of 'certainty'. This too is misconceived. Certainty is a psychological state that one can be in independently of whether or not one knows or justifiably believes that p. The falsity of p is no barrier to one's feeling certain that p is the case. Religious beliefs, the conviction that a given horse will win the next race, and many similar instances, amply demonstrate this. The original conflation of the subjective psychological state of certainty

_____

2   Descartes, *Meditations*; see Meditation 1; Russell, *The Problems of Philosophy*, 1912, chapter 1.

with the possession of a secure basis of knowledge is an arte-fact of Descartes' way of constructing the epistemological task. In his view, the task was to provide a secure route to knowledge from a subjective origin, *viz.* the origin or view-point of the knowing subject's own private data of con-sciousness. From these subjective data a route had to be found, supported by the right kind of epistemological collat-eral, to a public world existing outside and independently of that consciousness. Since the knowing subject himself had to be able to sort the contents of his consciousness into those that merited being called knowledge, from those that did not merit the label – that is: since the knowing subject had to be able to be sure that these items were knowledge, whereas those were (say) merely dreams – the mark of knowledge from the subjective viewpoint was thus the nature of the psychological mode of its entertainment, *viz.* a feeling of certainty.

Nearly all of Descartes' successors in epistemology, up to and including Russell and Ayer, shared this view that the starting point for epistemology lies in subjective experience, and therefore faced the same difficulty in securing the epis-temic guarantees for at least some of that experience which would rebut sceptical challenges. As with Descartes himself, doubtless the conceptual elision between certainty as a psy-chological attitude and certainty as a property of founda-tional or otherwise indubitable truths played its part in this. But in any case, certainty is not the target in epistemology, and if it appears in the residue of showing how to meet sceptical challenges it will be because the kind of epistemic assurance thus provided has, as an expected epiphenomenon, that attendant psychological attitude.

As noted, sceptical challenges inform us that we suffer an epistemic plight; namely, that we can have the best evidence for claiming to know that p, and yet be wrong. Scepticism thus demonstrates the existence of a gap between the grounds a putative knower has for some claim, and the claim itself. Traditional responses to scepticism take the form of attempts either to bridge or close the gap. The standard perceptual model, in which beliefs are formed by sensory interaction with the world, together with ratiocination upon the data thus gleaned, postulates a causal bridge across the gap as the basis of knowledge. Given the vulnerability of the bridge to sceptical sabotage, the causal story requires support of some kind.

So do other bridges over the gap – inferential ones, as (again for a prime example) in the Cartesian epistemological tradition. Descartes identified the epistemology's task as the need to specify a guarantee – call it X for the moment – which, added to our subjective grounds for our beliefs, protects them against sceptical challenge and thereby elevates them into knowledge. His candidate for X was the goodness (the goodness, not merely the existence) of a deity – for a good deity's goodness would ensure that it would not wish us to be misled by what appears to be evidence – so long as we use our epistemic endowments responsibly. The mere existence of a deity is insufficient; it might, as Descartes' own evil demon hypothesis suggests, be a mischievous deity, thereby guaranteeing the unreliability of our beliefs instead.

Some of those of Descartes' successors who accepted his starting point (henceforth, the Cartesian starting point) likewise sought an X to support the inferences from subjective experience to an independent and objective world, but not all of them felt able to invoke a divinity for the task. Yet others sought not to bridge the gap but to close it; this was the strategy of Berkeley and of the phenomenalists. In Berkeley's view, problems arise from thinking that behind or beyond experience there is a material world, where 'material' is a technical philosophical term denoting an empirically undetectable substance existentially supporting the sensible properties of things. Berkeley rejected the concept of matter (he did not reject the existence of the physical world) on the grounds of its empirical undetectability and the fact that sensible properties can, *qua* experienced entities, only have as their substance what is capable of experiencing them, *viz.* mind – and thereby closed the putative gap between experience and the world, for the latter turns out to consist in the former.

The phenomenalists made a similar move, with the interesting and more complicated difference that whereas for Berkeley all existence is actual (because everything is always actually perceived by the divine mind), most existence for the phenomenalists is merely possible – for the world is a (logical, in Russell) construction out of sensibilia, by which is meant actual and possible sense-data. Thus all those things not currently perceived by anyone exist as possibilities of perception (in Mill: a physical object is a permanent possibility of sensation). In being committed to the bare truth of an infinity of counterfactual conditionals, phenomenalism is therefore less tidy than Berkeleian idealism, in which all counterfactuals (which have a use only for finite minds: 'If I were in my study I would see my books') are cashed in terms of what is actually the case from the infinite mind's point of view. (It was once thought that one gets phenomenalism from Berkeley merely by subtracting God; this is incorrect – one has to add an ontology of possibilia and with it a commitment to the bare truth of counterfactuals.)

These gap-bridging or gap-closing endeavours all assume, more or less directly, the Cartesian starting point, and their familiar failure to provide satisfactory responses to the sceptical challenge accordingly suggests, among other things, that there is something deeply suspect about that starting point. In their different ways Wittgenstein and Dewey both argued that the epistemological enterprise should start in the public domain, not in the privacy of individual consciousness – Dewey nominates the participant perspective, Wittgenstein's private language argument appears to subvert the notion of a Cartesian starting point altogether. It does so because a private language is what a Cartesian subject requires in order to discourse about the inner contents of his mental life. A private language, in Wittgenstein's sense, is one that is available only to one speaker, not as a contingent but a logical fact: no one can share the language with that speaker even in principle. Wittgenstein's argument to the incoherence of this notion is this: language is a rule-governed activity, and one only succeeds in speaking a language if one follows the rules for the use of its expressions. But a solitary would-be language-user would not be able to tell the difference between actually following the rules and merely believing that he is doing so; so the language he speaks cannot be logically private to himself. It must be shared – and can indeed only be acquired, in the first place – in a public setting.[3]

The anti-sceptical possibilities of the private-language argument did not seem to be apparent to Wittgenstein himself, for later, in his notes 'On Certainty', he employs a more traditional response to scepticism, somewhat in the tradition of Hume and Kant, by saying that there are some things we simply have to accept in order to get on with our ordinary ways of thinking and speaking. Such propositions as that there is an external world, or that the world came into existence a long time ago, are not open to doubt; it is not an option for us to question them, because they constitute the

---

3   The points here are widely discussed in the literature. In Wittgenstein the locus classicus is *Philosophical Investigations* I, 80–242 (esp. 143–242).

framework of the discourse within which more particular claims of knowledge and expressions of doubt make sense. Wittgenstein calls them 'grammatical' propositions – thereby according them a constitutive, sense-fixing or practice-fixing role – and described them figuratively as the 'scaffolding' of our ordinary thought and talk; or, varying his metaphor, as the bed and banks of the river of our discourse.[4]

Whatever one makes of the quasi-foundationalism of Wittgenstein's approach in 'On Certainty', its similarity to its forerunners in Hume and Kant is suggestive, and prompts one to remember that part of Kant's aim in arguing that our cognitive structures play an essential constitutive role in shaping how the world appears to us, is precisely to address the 'scandal of philosophy', which as he saw it was its inability hitherto to reply adequately to sceptical challenges.

The thesis turns on a transcendental argument to the conditions of the possibility of experience. Its interest lies in arguing that minds are so constituted that they impose a framework of interpretative concepts upon our sensory input, among them those of the objectivity and causal interconnectedness of what we perceive. Application of these

---

4   See A. C. Grayling, 'Wittgenstein on Scepticism and Certainty', Chapter 4 above; and 'Wittgenstein's Influence: Meaning, Mind and Method', in Griffiths, *Wittgenstein Centenary Essays*, Cambridge University Press, 1991.

concepts transforms mere passive reception of sensory input into experience properly so called. Kant added the thought that our faculties are such that when raw data comes under the interpreting activity of our application of concepts, they have already had spatial and temporal form conferred upon them by the nature of our sensory capacities. The point is that if the sceptic asks how we are justified in claiming knowledge, then even if his claim relates to some specific matter rather than to the possibility of knowledge in general, the justificatory explanation will quickly come to rest on the foundation thus provided: we believe what we do because we must, at peril of failing to be able to have experience at all.

Prescinding from the details of Kant's endeavour, it is arguable that the strategy has much to recommend it, and it has been worked out in more detail both by the present writer and P. F. Strawson.[5] Strawson was criticized by Stroud and others for having smuggled a verification principle into his version of the Kantian transcendental argument; my defence of the strategy consists in describing the foundational beliefs identified by such argument as undischargeable assumptions of our conceptual scheme. If that manoeuvre is right, it shifts the sceptic's position from a challenge about justification to a challenge over the question whether the

---

5   P. F. Strawson, *Individuals*, Routledge, 1959; P. F. Strawson, *The Bounds of Sense*, 1965; A. C. Grayling, *The Refutation of Scepticism*, esp. chapters 3 and 4.

conceptual scheme is the only one possible – for if it is not, then ultimate security for the practice of making knowledge claims is still lacking since the claims in question are only justified parochially to the given scheme. The task then is to show that it does indeed make sense to talk only of one conceptual scheme (on Davidson's grounds – perhaps, indeed, that 'the very idea of a conceptual scheme' is itself empty if there can only be one). And this is to say that arguing against scepticism thus, and finally, takes the form of arguing against relativism.

So the claim being made here is this: properly anatomized, scepticism is a challenge, in a given area of discourse, to justify the epistemic grounds we assume or employ in that discourse. The motivations (the sceptical considerations adduced) identify where the positive task of justification is to be carried out. To shift attention to relativism as the last resort of the sceptic, it is necessary to make out more fully the claim that invoking facts about our frameworks of discourse (the conceptual scheme presupposed to given types of epistemic activities) settles the sceptical challenge at the level at which it has been traditionally pitched.

The intuition from which to begin is that one cannot know or believe just one thing. A commonplace belief about some object or state of affairs in the world comes as a component of a network of beliefs between which there are complex relations of support and dependency. Questions about these relations, especially about those which provide justification for particular knowledge claims, are among the most important in epistemology. An idea worth examining, therefore, is that the network of beliefs constitutes an implicit inference-licensing scheme, in which specifiable general beliefs play something like a foundational role and in which a particular pattern of inference (I shall suggest that it is deductive inference on something like the covering-law model) is dominant. Each of the points here requires examination.

The expression 'foundational role' has just occurred. A characteristic shortcoming of foundationalist theories of any kind is their failure to yield satisfactory explanations of the relation between what they respectively identify as basis and superstructure in the epistemic edifice. Across a range of proposals there is little persuasive detail about the logical mechanisms by which these different candidates for the role of conceptual support play their part. A promising model of this relationship is suggested by the concept of a 'covering law', the idea being that an assertion about some particular matter is legitimate when its being inferable from a description of its grounds is a result of that inference's being licensed by our conceptual commitments for that region of interest, in the form of one or more covering generalizations. More fully, the idea is that certain assumptions serve as inference-licensers which stand to particular inferences either in the direct relation of a major premise, or as setting the terms in which particular arguments are permitted to count as sound in the standard logical sense. This intuition seems promising; the task is to make it out more fully.

The strategy is to argue that finitary constraints on our capacities as investigators prompt the need for a conceptual framework which enables us to mitigate the restrictions they impose. The two tasks confronting us at the outset are (a) to specify the constitution of the framework, and (b) to describe the relations between the framework and particular beliefs deployed in our ordinary epistemic practice. Because of the enormous practical difficulties of carrying out these tasks, an appropriate starting point is to explore some possibilities for constructing a *model* which conservatively satisfies (a) and (b) together. The model is conservative because it attempts to specify the relationships at issue in (b) in standard logical terms, and because the commitments at issue in (a) are thought of, as uncontroversially as possible, in this familiar way: as the belief that there are causally interactive particulars (and events involving them) occupying space and, whether or not they are objects of thought or experience while doing so, persisting through stretches of time. Because of the causal character of the relations between the elements of this ontology, we can be regarded as assuming also that the physical realm is nomological in character, a fact which allows us to place a high degree of confidence in the regularities we take it to display. This picture is straightforwardly realist, the key to its being so lying in our commitment to the independent existence and character of the realm over part of which we take our thought and experience to range. The rest we take to be concealed from view, its constituents inaccessible to us either in fact or in principle, depending upon the manner in which they transcend our investigatory capacities.

At this level of generality the description is neutral with respect to finer-grained metaphysical issues, in particular the questions whether there are other things beside concrete spatio–temporal items, and whether some or all of these latter should be thought of as events rather than particulars. On the question of causal laws, however, something more definite is implied by the suggestions to follow.

Certain commonplaces about our limitations as individual epistemic agents, together with certain other commonplaces about our powers in the same respect, offer to explain the role of the first order realist assumptions just nominated as constituting the (model) framework, as follows.

It is an all too familiar fact that the epistemic capacities of humans are finite. We suffer the 'finitary predicament'; our empirical resources for acquiring and testing information about the world are limited, and so are our powers of inference, analysis, recognition and memory.

A standard way of dramatizing this predicament is to reflect on the circumstances of a lifelong solitary and in particular the question of what he might construct for himself in the way of a world-view with nothing available to him beyond his native cognitive equipment. There are several such models in the recent literature of epistemology, including influential suggestions by Russell, Strawson and Ayer.[6] But one must guard against the failure to distinguish between different notions here: that of the *egocentric* predicament (the epistemically solipsistic predicament) which is what a true solitary would suffer, and the *finitary* predicament, which is suffered even by members of a community who share a language and pool their epistemic resources. If the notion of an egocentric predicament makes sense, it does so as a species of finitary predicament, for although what is central to its being effectively a form of solipsism is the individual's isolation, the problem which this renders insurmountable is the limited character of the individual's native cognitive resources; that is, his epistemic finitude. But there is good reason to think that talk of an egocentric predicament fails to make sense. This is because it turns on the idea of a wholly subjective perspective, in which the subject is supposed to recognize his perspective as his own without having any way of locating it in a setting of other perspectives, since these *ex hypothesi* do not exist. And this is controversial: for it would seem that the notion of a sense of self, or at least of a sustained centre of experience which in

6   The main example is A. J. Ayer's in *The Central Questions of Philosophy*, Weidenfeld & Nicolson, 1973, chapter V. Strawson essays the construction of a purely auditory world in the first part of *Individuals*.

some sense recognizes that experience as its own, cannot be rendered intelligible independently of systematic relations to other such perspectives – other selves – and this implies that to be a self is necessarily to be a member of a community of such things. Among other things, membership of such a community seems to be a necessary condition for acquisition of the scheme, best thought of as embodied in language as the base theory its semantics requires, and by reference to which such experience is enjoyed.

But recognizing that the notion of an egocentric predicament is incoherent does not diminish the demands made on our epistemology by the fact of epistemic finitude. Here, what is crucial is that even as members of a co-operative we suffer sharp finitary constraints on our epistemic capacities, and the dramatization of that predicament which the egocentric case affords serves only to identify a gap in need of filling: the gap between what any individual might be imagined capable of constructing by way of a world-view on his own account, and the contents of the conceptual scheme we in fact possess.

Recognizing both the existence and character of the gap is what, as noted, forces the abandonment of the Cartesian perspective in epistemology. According to that perspective our privileged access to the data of our own consciousnesses, and their incorrigibility, is what is supposed in large part to underwrite our confidence in what they convey. The sceptical challenges – based on what opens the gap, and renders it unbridgeable; namely, the considerations about perceptual relativities, psychological contingencies, test cases like deception by a evil demon, and the mediate and inferential nature of perception itself – are responsible for this; they are in effect fatal to Cartesian epistemology.

But there are still lessons to be learned from examining the gap which Cartesian epistemologists tried in so many ingenious ways to bridge or close. The lessons flow from trying to answer the question posed above, and which in fuller form runs: if we take seriously the fact that the cognitive capacities of individuals are limited, what follows for an understanding of the global theories we formulate and employ concerning the objects of those capacities? That is: how, given their epistemic limitations, do individuals come to have and use a shared theory of the world with putatively inclusive ambitions – namely, our commonsense conceptual scheme as adjusted and supplemented by science? What status can we suppose that scheme to have, given its radical underdetermination by the evidence which subscribers to it can acquire in the course of activities bearing upon the verification or falsification of the beliefs constituting it?

There is a platitudinous but rather vague answer, already suggested. It is that our sharing a conceptual scheme which none of us individually could have generated, is a function of our belonging to a community whose chief instrument of community is language. Communal possession of language plays the major role in enabling community members to apportion epistemic tasks, to process and record the results, and to put them to use. There is no suggestion here that there cannot be any sort of shared conceptual scheme in the absence of language, for manifestly there are good naturalistic accounts to be given of languageless creatures displaying concept-applying behaviour in common with others of their kind, frequently in ways indispensable to their co-operative interactions. But we have no reason to suppose that a non-language-mediated conceptual scheme has complexity above a certain level, and it is barely controversial that the one we (humans) possess would be impossible without language.

It would not strictly be incorrect to describe the finitary predicament in terms of the deficiency or incompleteness of our information relative to our practical epistemic needs, in particular our having to choose courses of action. This is a formulation from which discussions of the ampliative character of induction often begin, and it serves as a statement of the dilemma posed by the joint fact of our pressing need for techniques of ampliative inference and their imperfection relative to deductive standards. But it would be, or at least could be, misleading to begin this way, because the problem which confronts us is not so much the deficiency of our state of information about the world as, at a quite different level, its completeness. At the level of detail – of particular matters – our knowledge is radically deficient. But at a highly general level there is a background of assumptions, some of a structural nature, against which our ordinary thought about the world proceeds and which makes it possible; and these jointly take the character of an overarching picture of the world which we hold steady as the interpretative frame for the first, deficient state of knowledge. It is the character of the overarching picture – the framework – and its relation to the latter, which invites attention here.

So: we are taking seriously the fact that the cognitive capacities of individuals are finite, and asking what follows from this for an understanding of the global theories we apply to the domains over which we exercise those capacities. This is not a question about *how*, in the light of epistemic finitude, individuals come to have and use a putatively inclusive explanatory theory of the world; rather, it is a question of *what work that theory – that conceptual scheme – does*. Privileging the second question over the first is something we have been taught by Kant to do: he pointed out that the crucial question concerns not how we get our concepts, but what role they play.

The question can be formulated in alternative ways to bring out others of the concerns which the fact of epistemic finitude prompts. For one important example, we can approach the task by asking what status we can suppose our conceptual scheme to have, given its radical underdetermination by the evidence which the subscribers to that scheme can acquire in the course of the activities which bear upon the verification or falsification of the commitments (the beliefs and theories) in which the scheme consists.

194

It is evident from the finitary character of individual cognitive powers that the conceptual scheme we employ would be at least extremely difficult to acquire – arguably: impossible to acquire – if it were left to individuals to construct it for themselves from their own resources – if the notion of such a proceeding were, in the light of the Private Language Argument, intelligible. The range of an individual's powers is restricted to his current perceptual environment and whatever of past experience and future expectation his limited powers of recall and inference can provide. Without supplement, these powers would (whether or not equally) at best very weakly support a large number of widely divergent interpretations of what they give their possessor access (or supposed access) to.

This shows the special interest of the discrepancy between the finitary predicament of any of us taken individually, and the richness of the conceptual scheme we each in fact employ. What makes possession of such a scheme possible? One ready and persuasive answer comes from reminding ourselves that we are not isolated individuals, but members of an epistemic community whose chief instrument of community is language. Language enables members of the community to share epistemic tasks and to process, record and utilize the results. There are certain obvious ways in which that process can be portrayed: Popper, for example, with a certain literal-mindedness, thinks of libraries (or, more generally, data banks of various kinds) as embodying the outcomes of the community's joint epistemic activities over time. This must be partly right. But what is more to the present point is that the central role of linguistic competence, in making possible the difference between a rich conceptual scheme and individual finitude, suggests that the key lies in what goes into possession of that competence. And the thought must be that linguistic competence *essentially* involves or instantiates a theory of the world which enables any speaker of the language to interpret, or indeed to have, experience of the world in that way. Another way to put this is to view linguistic competence as a sixth epistemic modality, where by 'epistemic modality' I mean a means of acquiring, interpreting, processing, storing and transmitting the information yielded by experience and reflection on experience. So considered, linguistic competence is a vastly more powerful epistemic modality than the five other, strictly sensory, modalities; it is what provides them with their framework of operation. What is needed is an account of the scheme instantiated by application of linguistic competence.

One thing we immediately recognize about the scheme is that, as already noted, it is realist in character. Despite appearances and much misleading debate, realism is an *epistemological* thesis asserting the independence of the objects of discourse from discourse itself. More precisely, it asserts that relations between thought and its objects, perception and its targets, knowledge and what is known, acts of referring and referents – call them 'mind-world' relations, although in fact they are all different if intimately connected – are external or contingent ones.

We can recognize, as fundamental to understanding the way in which our discourse works, assumptions of the kind listed earlier about the world being a law-governed realm of causally interacting spatio–temporal particulars, and events or other entities typically individuated by reference to these. Moreover, commitments in these respects reveal why ordinary discourse invites accounts of reference and truth which are distinctively realist, for a view of the foregoing kind about the domain over which our discourse ranges is very naturally interpretable in terms of those familiar views about the links between referring devices and things, and between sentences and objectively obtaining truth-conditions, which are presupposed to much recent discussion in this area: namely, that reference works on a naming-paradigm in causally direct ways, and that truth in some sense consists in the fit between what we say or think about the domain over which discourse ranges, and the domain itself.

Whatever particular difficulties affect giving an exact account of the ontology and the semantics invited by this realist picture, it is at least clear that it constitutes a simple and powerful view which on the whole successfully sustains the demands made on it by experience – a strong pragmatic justification for it. That is a fact which is independent of debates about whether the realist commitments of the scheme are *literally true* or not, a question upon which much turns; but for present purposes they can be left aside, because we need only note that we are construing the commitments weakly *as assumptions* of the scheme. Whether they are taken as literally true or merely as assumptions, the scheme's justificatory character remains. It becomes a matter for the second task, identified earlier, to settle this question of 'literal truth'; that is, how these first-order facts about the scheme are to be interpreted in the light of the sceptical problem which gives that second task its content.[7]

Collecting the suggestions already made, we can venture the following as a first approximation of what the framework of ordinary epistemic practice looks like, treated as a justificatory scheme. Such a scheme is in effect an inferential scheme, representable as providing security for familiar practices of basing judgements on evidence. In standard thinking about these matters, empirical judgements are thought of as inductively based on the evidence for them, and as being defeasible to the degree that the evidence is partial. But we have just noted that the scheme consists of a set of assumptions about the nature of the world over which our experience ranges, and we have further noted that these assumptions include some to the effect that the world is

---

7   Many complex issues arise here: for one treatment of them see
    A. C. Grayling, 'Epistemology and Realism', *Proc. Arist. Soc.*,
    1992.

lawlike and independent. Add these assumptions to statements of evidence as supporting premises, and the logical
picture changes: we see that the form of reasoning being
employed is enthymematic deduction on the covering-law
model.

At its roughest, the picture is something like this. A judgement about some particular matter of fact is inferred from
the evidence for that judgement (reported by *evidential premises*) in the presence of more general premises about the
kinds of things in question, and even more general standing
premises about the world (*background premises*). As such, the
form of reasoning is representable as deductive: the conjunction of evidential and background premises entails the judgement. But, of course, empirical judgements are defeasible,
which appears to conflict with the idea that inferences to
them take deductive form. The answer lies in noting, first,
that background premises have to carry *ceteris paribus* clauses,
or clauses about normal conditions; and second, that evidential premises are only as good as the evidence they report,
and here the usual finitary constraints apply. Accordingly we
can be, and often enough we are, wrong in our judgements.
But we can often measure the degree of confidence that we
repose in our judgements, by taking into account the relevant defeating possibilities inherent in either or both the
evidence that evidential premises report, and the stability of
the normal conditions assumed in background premises.
This is where this picture saves what is persuasive about

199

conceptions of probability, and in effect 'solves the problem of induction' by suggesting that all reasoning is always deductive in form. (For example, inferences by analogy assume uniformity of nature grounds – and so for other non-enumerative inductive forms.)

It is illuminating to think of Aristotelian classification as, obliquely, among the forerunners of this idea of an inferential scheme. Two reasons why there is only heuristic value in remarking the connection are these: the Aristotelian system of classification by genus and species is too neat (too simplistic) even for the domain where it has most plausibility – namely, the biological domain; and second, discussion of it came to be distracted, perhaps not unnaturally, into discussion of definition, and in that guise the objections to it are many and obvious. Some are tellingly summarized by Locke in the *Essay* (not every term can be precisely explained by two other terms giving genus and differentia; and some words cannot be lexically defined, on pain among other things of regress and failure to constrain their meanings by reference to extra-linguistic considerations).[8] But there is much that is suggestive there (and in later logic: see the Kneales on medieval theories of assumption). Note, for example, the striking resemblance between the Tree of Porphyry and the structure of reasoning

---

8   Questions of definition range more widely than this; in the early debate the tendency was to approximate the analytic rather than the 'in use' end of the spectrum.

employed in the game of Twenty Questions, in which moderately skilled questioners can identify any individual spatio–temporal object usually in fewer than 20 steps, exploiting classificatory conventions governing our picture of the world together with appropriate cognitive strategies. What both seem to capture is the sense that inferences about matters of fact proceed to their conclusions by way of the deductive inferential structure outlined: premises of relatively great generality are conjoined with premises of relatively lesser generality, including particular ones, in any number of steps within practical constraints, to yield, in a highly reliable way even in the face of defeasibility considerations, judgements about matters of fact.

These remarks are merely schematic, and only gesture in the direction of a research programme. But the implications of such an approach are clear. The quest for an account of justification is satisfied by this picture, as explaining how it consists in inherence in a scheme or framework. Full statements of justification proceed, via a report of the relevant evidence in the case, to appeal to the scheme as a whole: 'This', we might in the end say in such a transaction, 'is how (we think) the world is', and that has to satisfy the sceptic at that level of enquiry. He might then – he should – raise his sights to the question of the justification of the scheme as a whole, but that, as noted, is a different and further matter. (Some, like Carnap and Wittgenstein in their different ways, would take it that there can be no such higher task.) But then the problem of scepticism comes to be seen as arguably it ought to be seen: as the problem of relativism.

The standard difficulties concerning justification can be taken implicitly to specify desiderata that have to be satisfied by any adequate theory of justification. They are not best satisfied by attempting to defeat the defeaters proposed by sceptical arguments of the familiar sort, as earlier epistemology often tried to do, not untypically on a blow-by-blow basis. Rather, they are satisfied by a positive theory which shows how justification is secured. A theory like the present one, which postulates ultimate justification by reference to the assumptions of the scheme, serving as foundational premises from which, together with other premises, judgements of lesser generality are deduced, accordingly satisfies these desiderata. It does so conditionally upon resolution of the higher-order question about the overall justification of the scheme itself, of course, which is where the determining connection of the first- to the second-order enterprises becomes manifest: it shows that something like a transcendental deduction of the assumptions of the scheme, together with an argument that any alternative scheme *can* only be a variant of this one (the modality is seriously intended), is required to deal with scepticism fully. Once again, this higher-order task is sometimes claimed to have been effected already in the lower-order one, on the grounds that only the lower-order one is possible anyway; but that is precisely one of the central controversies of recent epistemology.

Among much else that might be said about the strategy outlined here, I shall mention in conclusion just one. In earlier debates about empirical knowledge it was pointed out that reasoning about matters of fact does not take the form of conjunctions of evidential and background premises entailing judgements. Judgements, especially perceptual ones, are typically immediate, appearing to consist in the exercise of well-rehearsed, experience-based recognitional capacities. As a description of how empirical judgement *feels* (so to speak), this is surely correct; but it involves a confusion of psychological and logical facts about its structure. True, we do not as a matter of psychological fact usually go through processes of inference in such cases; but we can see that if challenged to justify a judgement we would have to state our grounds and, if pressed, the background assumptions that constitute them as grounds. In a full story of this kind we would have the conceptual scheme *qua* inferential framework fully present, and would be able to trace inferential routes to the judgement itself.

The nub of the claim here is that we can redescribe the problem of justification as the problem of epistemic finitude, and, by seeing how such finitude is overcome – *viz.* by our possession and employment of a realistic conceptual scheme which serves as a geographical–historical explanatory framework designed to make experience coherent, serving as a framework of inference, specifically deductive in form, in which the general assumptions of the scheme play an undischargeable role – we thereby see how we come by justification for our workaday epistemic judgements. And we thereby also identify where the major philosophical task in this region lies: namely, in justifying the scheme itself, which is the same thing as refuting scepticism in its most interesting and substantial guise – namely, as relativism. This is a *different* problem of justification, but it only comes to the fore when epistemology's traditional problem of justification has been dealt with in the way suggested here.

Index

Index